SHUT THE F*CK UP AND LISTEN (MORE)

Shut the F*ck Up and Listen (More)

Stop Talking and Start Connecting

Eric Oberembt

Published by Game Changer Publishing

Paperback ISBN: 978-1-966659-55-6

Hardcover ISBN: 978-1-966659-56-3

Digital ISBN: 978-1-966659-57-0

www.GameChangerPublishing.com

I want to dedicate this book to my late grandfather, Delton Mares. My grandfather was my person. He believed in me when no one else did. I had many people doubt me in my life, and I'm sure there were times when he had concerns. But he was always there. No matter what. In my darkest times, he stood by me and believed in me. Without him, I wouldn't have the amazing family I have today. I wouldn't have the belief system I have today. He truly helped mold me into who I have become.

I want to say thank you to my wife, Natalie. She has never seen me drunk or high. She has been lucky to only get this version of Eric. But she has changed who I am as a person, and I couldn't have written this book without her support. She helped me learn how to be healthy again and take care of ourselves. We have been through a lot over twelve years together, and no matter how tough it got, she stuck around. I couldn't do all the things I do on a daily basis in my business and all my crazy ass ideas without her support and belief in me.

To my daughter, Teegan. I love you so much. You have changed my life and how I see the world and people around me. You have made me want to be a better person so that I can make sure you become the best human you can become. I hope you are proud of the man your dad has become and will continue to strive to be. I would literally die for you. You are my world.

From left to right: Eric, Natalie, and Teegan (9)

READ THIS FIRST

Just to say thanks for buying and reading my book, I would like to give you an opportunity to check out our accountability group "Cult Culture Movement" for free!

Attend one call and see if you are a fit for the group. No one will try to sell you anything. I formed this group for entrepreneurs looking for people to hold them accountable for their lives.

Scan the QR Code Here:

SHUT THE F*CK UP AND LISTEN (MORE)

STOP TALKING AND START CONNECTING

ERIC OBEREMBT

FOREWORD

By Steve D. Sims
Entrepreneur, Author, Speaker

When I first met Eric Oberembt, I wasn't sure what to expect. He's loud, direct, and doesn't pull punches. But once you get past the bluntness, you find something rare: a man who genuinely gives a damn about people. And that's why Eric's story is worth paying attention to.

He's been through the trenches—addiction, failure, heartbreak—and clawed his way back. His lessons aren't pulled from motivational seminars or self-help jargon. They were earned the hard way, through pain, setbacks, and the raw drive to rebuild himself. I've watched Eric transform his life and the lives of those he leads, and that's why when he talks, I shut up and listen.

This book will challenge you to dig deep. Eric's T.E.A.M. Method—Trust, Empathy, Authenticity, and Meaning—isn't just theory; it's a blueprint for building unshakable teams and a more fulfilling life. It'll push you to *shut the f*ck up and listen*—not just to others, but to yourself. If you're ready to get real and make meaningful change, then dive in.

Trust me, Eric's the guide you want for this journey.

– Steve

FOREWORD

By Mark Lundholm
Comedian, Author, Actor, Father

This book has a lot of heart. It also has very sharp teeth. Eric Oberembt takes an unflinching look at healthy relationships, personal growth, business practices and tactics, and community standards that seem to shift with the times. His savvy narrative and keen advice are based on his own experience, drive, and commitment to better! I have always known him to be a man who is ethical, empathetic, incredibly honest and, above all, true to his word. I see all of that and more in this book. Manhood, brotherhood, fatherhood, and being a contributing member of a neighborhood... This book outlines a path of "good hood": LISTEN-LEARN-LEAD—quite a destination for some, a solid invitation for others, and an impossible goal for most.

Wanna be one of the few who attain the rare air of personal excellence? Keep reading, my friend.

Safe travels along the way,

– Mark

CONTENTS

INTRODUCTION

"Who in the world am I? Ah, that's the great puzzle."
– Alice's Adventures in Wonderland

Some call it destiny, others call it fate—but what if your calling was already pulsing through your veins from a young age? I know mine was. My name is Eric Oberembt, a third-generation business owner who knew early on that roofing would be my money maker. I've been with my roofing company, D&M Roofing and Siding, for over thirty years—first as an employee when I was a kid and now as the CEO and one-hundred-percent owner. I literally started roofing when I was ten years old. I lived with my grandfather, Delton Mares, starting when I was seven.

By the time I was ten, he had me up on flat commercial buildings, ripping off old tar and gravel roofs. I was running a tar kettle by the time I was fourteen and sold my first job when I was sixteen.

I always knew that roofing was the business I wanted to be in, but I also knew I didn't want to work as HARD as my grandfather did. I wanted to work smarter, not harder, but I had no idea how to do that, so I watched him. I watched others. I asked questions. I started going to conferences, trade shows, and seminars and joining masterminds. I spent a shitload of money trying to learn more about business, and let me tell you, the five years I spent drinking and f*cking off in college did not prepare me to run one.

Delton D. Mares 4/21/33–6/23/2015 (My best friend)

I quit college because I couldn't find a parking space, by the way. I was on my third school, driving around campus for over an hour, trying to find somewhere to park so some asshole who had never actually run a business could teach me "business ethics." *Ugh*... Can I say how much I f*cking hate college professors as a general rule? I realize there are a ton of good ones. Trust me, I know that. But overall, they are pompous assholes. None of them have done shit but read a book. That shit drives me nuts. That's how fed up I got with institutional education: I quit school because of a parking space.

After my failed search, I called Gramp and told him I was done with school and wanted him to give me more appointments to run. He asked one time if I was sure. I told him that I was, and he said, "You got it. See ya later tonight." That was how I quit school and went all in on business.

I have now grown our company from generating a maximum of two hundred thousand dollars in annual revenue to a successful multimillion-dollar entity operating in multiple states. To be clear, that took me f*cking up a lot of times—like, *a lot* of times. But every time I did, I decided that was my tuition. That was the real education I needed to be paying for.

I'm most proud of the numerous people I've employed over the years and how working for D&M Roofing has changed their lives and mine. The biggest compliment I've ever been given is when people move on from my company to go somewhere else and tell me that being at my organization taught them the things that they needed to have the courage to take the next step in their journey. I realize that my company is not EVERYONE's final destination. Now, I hope it is for some, but I know that it's not for everyone. My goal is to help them become who they are meant to be, and if that means they fulfill that destiny at D&M, awesome. If it's somewhere else, cool. There's no bigger compliment in life than that for me.

When this happened to me a couple of times, it made me realize I had done something right. I didn't really know what it was, but I knew that I had figured out a way to connect with people. I realized that I had made an impact on people's lives through my company and the ecosystem I had created.

I now realize that a lot of the knowledge that I gained and have put into my organization comes from the tools and skills I received from getting sober. As of the writing of this book, I have been free of all drugs and alcohol for fifteen years (but who's counting?). I learned why I drank. I learned why I was always living in fear. I learned why I hid in the corner, unable to work up the courage to talk to anyone unless I downed a handle of vodka and did an "eight-ball" of cocaine. I learned I was yearning for acceptance and connection. I'm sure you can't relate to that at all, right?

When I realized what I was missing in life and the substitute I was using to try to find it... I knew something had to change. You'll hear some of my stories in this book about when I was a real piece of shit. You won't hear all of them. The cost of admission for those is a little steeper, but you'll hear the ones that got me here.

The reason I mention all of this is that I want people to know they aren't alone. Yes, this is technically a business book. I'm going to teach you some shit you can do to create a better culture in your company. When you do, your people will become higher performers, and your company will thrive. BUT... I really want to make sure I also connect with anyone reading this book who feels lost and alone and doesn't know where to turn.

That doesn't mean you're an alcoholic. It could. But it could be that you're just depressed as shit because you don't have anyone that gets you. They don't get what you're going through. They don't know what it's like to be a high-performing MF-er and what it takes to strive for that every day.

Well, I do. A lot of us do. We have to surround ourselves with those people. That's why I started the Cult Culture Movement Coaching Group—so that guys and gals like me could have a place to go to just be "ok," a place where we could hold each other accountable for our shit, share wins and losses, and help each other grow. So the point is that you're not alone. You have no excuse. If you choose to hide, take on everything on your own, and not make changes, it's on you.

In the last few years, I have been given some amazing opportunities to speak on stage and share my T.E.A.M. Method and my story of recovery. Let me tell you, there is nothing I enjoy more. I love being able to share with an audience how you can change your life and the lives of others just by paying attention. This book is based on the things I teach in my coaching group and speak about on stage. But y'all will get a few more fun stories. :)

I host a successful podcast called *Be Authentic or Get the F*ck Out*. I use this platform to have real conversations with folks I want to know better. I'm super selfish about it. Lol. I literally get to sit and talk with people for over an hour and learn about their lives and how they have overcome adversity. Then, I can take that knowledge and apply it to my life. The cool part is... so can my listeners.

Along with the community I already told you about, the Cult Culture Movement, I am the facilitator of a mastermind retreat that is focused on facing fears and doing the thing that I love the most: scuba diving. It's called the Underwater Mastermind "Exhale." Clever, huh? We do the trip twice a year and take applications about six months in advance. If diving is something you love or would like to find out if you love, hit me up.

I've been to jail and faced multiple years in prison. I've had multiple divorces. I've been unhealthy and overweight—three hundred ten pounds, fat as shit... Then, I found my way and my people to change all of those things. I got where I am today because of the people who helped me. That's why I wrote this book—so it can help YOU.

I got here because people believed in me when I didn't believe in myself. My grandfather was the most instrumental. He didn't even give up on me when I was spending thirty days in rehab. He came up and stayed with me to see what I was going through. He believed in me. At the time, I had no idea why, but I think he would be proud today.

I just kept talking to people. I kept making connections and relationships.

Getting clean was the best thing that ever happened to me, and it has given me the life that I have today. I wrote this book because I wanted to speak to myself fifteen years ago. I want to speak to people who feel like they don't know how to connect with others. They might know how to be successful with money but sometimes feel like they're still hiding in the shadows. They're looking for ways to get all of their people to find a higher purpose and connect with each other.

This book is for anyone who's ever felt lonely. (So, pretty much everyone...? Yes.) It's for anyone who wants to build a better team and culture in their company and at home. This book is for the unfulfilled leader inside. I'm not going to expound on this much because anyone who is in a leadership position in business or at home can gain from this book.

Now, why should you listen to me? Great f*cking question. I'll be honest. Sometimes, I have to ask myself that as well. (Imposter syndrome— ever heard of it?) The best line I ever heard was from my friend Brian Galke, who said on my podcast that the only people who don't have imposter syndrome are imposters. Well said, Brian. Well said.

I have hired and fired tons of people. I've learned the hard way what makes a good employee and what doesn't. I have also figured out that I tend to keep people around for too long because I think I can fix them. Shocker... I can't, generally. I have learned through my last twenty years in business the right way and the wrong way to treat people. To be clear, I still make mistakes. I still screw up with people. I still say the wrong thing. I say the wrong thing a lot, actually. Here is the difference. Today, I catch it. Fast. Then, I correct it. That's the definition of a good leader. When you f*ck up, what do you do? Do you correct it?

I've learned how to get people to totally believe in you and know that what you say is true. If you can do this, they will follow you to the gates of hell. Once you figure that out, the rest is easy. Keep in mind that I did it wrong for many years as well.

What you're going to get out of my book is how to build a high-producing team inside of your organization so you can create extreme wealth not only for you but for the people in that organization, financially and emotionally. I'm far more passionate about the emotional side of it. I want people to be okay with who they are and not have to pretend to be somebody else—hence, the "Authentic" in the podcast title.

If you're able to be exactly who you are, all the financial shit will come after that. I hope that after reading this book, everyone takes the things that I have learned over the years and all the pain and shit that I've been through, implements it immediately in their lives, and becomes truly fulfilled in life, business, and their relationships.

None of this matters if we can't connect with our people. Give them the opportunity to feel lighter and supported, knowing that they have a network of trusted people to turn to for help. Let them know that it's easy for them to reach out because, when they open up, they'll be met with understanding and encouragement that strengthens their connections and drives them to even greater success.

I'm super excited to be able to walk this journey with you. I believe in you and what you can do, and I hope you enjoy the journey ahead.

ONE

TRUST

*"Trust is the glue of life. It's the most essential ingredient
in effective communication. It's the foundational
principle that holds all relationships."*
– Stephen R. Covey

Back in 2018, I was invited to go on a scuba diving trip in the Bahamas. The trip revolved around diving with tiger sharks.

Now, I've dove with sharks before. I've dove with reef sharks. I chased after some hammerheads in Hawaii. I've been around lemon sharks and all kinds of different types of sharks, but I'd never dove with tiger sharks. Before I went on this trip, I did some research on tiger sharks and discovered that they can weigh up to five hundred pounds. I also found out that their teeth are so sharp and their jaws so powerful that they can chew through bones. In fact, they're called the "trash cans of the sea." So, when I found all this out, I got excited and shit down my leg a little bit at the same time. But I showed up down in Palm Beach and got on a boat.

I would be living on this boat for seven days with around twenty other people. Oh… I forgot to tell you. I don't really like groups of people and am a natural introvert. So, I was freaking the f*ck out. I knew two other people on this boat and was already anxious as hell. We took an eight-hour boat trip overnight (I'll be honest, I have no idea if it was eight hours. But it felt like eight hours) to this place called Tiger Beach, somewhere in the middle of the ocean north of the Bahamas.

The next morning, we are on the boat, and they get everybody set up. They had told us all before we showed up what kind of gear to bring, and they'd said that we had to be completely blacked out. So we had to have a black wetsuit, a black hood, black gloves, and black fins. You didn't want colors because... fish are colorful. And fish... are food. And everything that I have is white, so I had to get all new stuff.

As we were getting geared up in the back of the boat, I looked over at the dive master who would be going down with us and saw that he had a giant cage full of chum—dead, bloody fish. The idea was that we would swim down and sit in a V formation on our knees on the bottom, about fifty feet down, with the current behind us. Then he would chum this cage up so that the blood, carried by the current, would get out into the open ocean, and tiger sharks and other sharks, which can smell the blood from a long way away, would then come running.

So, as the dive master is getting his chum bucket ready, I also look to see what kind of gear he's putting on, and it's f*cking chain mail like from medieval times. He looked like he was getting ready to go joust for a fair maiden's honor. He had chain mail on his head, like a hat, on his arms, and on his legs. And I was sitting there in a wetsuit only. He also had a bucket and was handing out one-inch white PVC sticks.

I asked him, "What exactly am I supposed to do with this PVC stick if a shark is coming at me? Am I supposed to jab at him? Is this to defend myself from a five-hundred-pound tiger shark?"

"No, no, no, no, no, no," he replied. "Do not poke at the sharks. They do not like to be poked."

I thought, *What the f*ck do you mean they don't like to be poked? Do they like to be tickled? Spoken softly to? Little pets under the chin? Why the hell are you giving me a Goddamn stick, then?*

Well... while you're sitting on your knees and watching these sharks come in over the reef, the purpose of the stick is that if they start to come at you, you hold firm with it. You don't lean, you don't poke, you just hold firm. If the shark hits the stick with his nose, he's going to know that you're not food, and he's going to veer off.

I looked at this guy and just went, "The f*ck they are." There's no way that this is my line of defense. There's no way that this is what is going to save my life.

Now, lo and behold, we jumped in, swam down to the bottom, and sat there with the tiger sharks. For the next two or three days, we did this.

On the last day, one of the big tiger sharks was coming my way. I stared at it, thinking, *No way. This thing is coming right at me. Why would she come right at me? I don't have anything she wants. I don't have any food. Wait... I am food... F*ck... Why is she still coming? She has to veer off... They always just veer off...* Nope. The damn thing kept coming. I stood firm with the one-inch white PVC stick. She bumped her nose... and veered off. Holy shit. That was intense.

What I learned was that, sometimes, you just have to trust. Sometimes, you have to trust that people know what they're talking about. You have to trust that people who have been there before will be able to lead you and that you'll be safe.

Trust is not given, though; it's earned. In that instance, that divemaster earned my trust. Really, he earned it for the rest of the trip based on him being right. So, what I really had was faith, I guess. I had faith and gave him trust because I knew that he knew more about these sharks than I did. I didn't have to be the smartest guy in the room or "on the boat." I just needed to shut the f*ck up and listen... But I thought he was crazy as shit when he told me what to do with that stick.

There are different ways to earn trust. You don't get it for just showing up.

I don't care if you're the friendliest guy in the world, buying everybody beers at the bar and making people laugh. You could be the most charming dude around, but that is not what is going to make people trust you. Trust is built over time, and it's built by actions.

You have to put in the work. You have to put in the effort to get people to believe in you one day at a time. If you think about it, you'll see that you don't just wake up and have people counting on you other than your children, right? But even with them, as they get older, you have to earn their trust, too. In the beginning, they just implicitly do, right? They don't really have a choice. Your job is to keep them alive, and they're trusting you to do that. But trust is built over time. There is no shortcut.

I like to use analogies with sports, and a good analogy for this is when you go to the gym: you can't just grab the heaviest weight and pump a set out right away. No, you've got to start with smaller weights, and you have to show up every single day. You have to get a little bit stronger every single day. One day, you'll show up and be able to do something that you never expected. Earning trust is the same way, right? You don't get to skip any steps.

Every action that you do, everything that you put into the world when you're dealing with your people in your office or at home, you have to do it day in and day out so they know that you're solid.

Another example of what I have forced myself to do and to make sure that I am aware of is if I say I'm going to do something, I make sure that I'm going to do it. For example, I could be working in my home office, and Teegan comes in and asks me to come out and play with her. I really want to go play with her, but I have to finish this thing that I'm doing, so I tell her, "Honey, give me fifteen minutes, and I'll come out."

Now, what am I going to do to make sure that no matter what, I keep my word on that fifteen minutes? I'm going to set an alarm because if I sit there for thirty minutes and she's waiting outside that door for me—sad because I broke my word—I start losing the trust of my own child. To me.....This is completely unacceptable. If breaking your word to your kid isn't on that non-negotiable list, you and I aren't going to get along.

Speaking of "keeping your word," this shit needs to come back into our lexicon and lifestyle. There was a time when the phrase actually meant something to people. It still means something to me. If I tell someone that I'm going to do something, I make damn sure I do it, even if it's not beneficial to me. I should have thought of that before I said I would do the thing. People don't have that honor anymore, and it really shows. People today don't even EXPECT people to keep their word. Everyone expects people to lie. Fake news... all that shit. No one believes anyone anymore. It's become the world we live in. I think it's sad. I challenge you to be different. Be the person who everyone knows is true to their word... no matter what. That's a difference-maker. That's the kind of shit that builds trust long-term.

Trust can be fragile. One wrong move, one lie, one broken promise, and bam, you're back to square one. It's like working out for ten years, getting into amazing shape, and then living on donuts and beer for a month. You'll watch all that hard work just melt away. Trust is the same way. It's fragile.

I know that sounds unfair, but that's life. That's how it is. Ask anyone who's screwed up big time in the public eye.

Look at Tiger Woods. He had people looking up to him from all over the world: kids, adults, everyone. Then came one big scandal, and his whole image was shattered. Nobody looked at him the same way. He's regained some of it, but everyone still looks at him a little sideways. If a story came out about him again, everyone would believe it regardless of whether it was true or not. Why? Because trust is that fragile. It took him years to get back into the good graces of the public.

What we're going to be talking about in this book is how to implement these different pillars of trust, empathy, authenticity, and meaning that I have coined as the "T.E.A.M. Method." If you use the T.E.A.M. Method, you will be able to build a team that trusts you, that you're able to connect with, and you're going to be able to raise them to levels that they never thought possible. *Trust* is the first pillar of that. If you don't have trust and if you're not striving to gain it, then none of the other stuff is going to matter.

Trust is the foundation of the house, and without a strong foundation, nothing that you build on it is going to matter. The other parts of the T.E.A.M. Method—and we'll get to those in later chapters—are built on this foundation.

You can have all kinds of different skills. You can be charming. You can have an amazing personality. If there are people in your life who don't trust you, it's pointless. How can you gain their trust?

Don't say you're going to be somewhere if you're not going to show up. Be on time. If you say you're going to be there at eight, be there at 7:55 because on time only lasts for a moment. Early lasts for a really long time, and late is anything after on time. Show up on time. I realize that everyone might talk about this... but can I repeat it again?

F*CKING BE ON TIME.

If you disrespect my time by not showing up when you said you would, we are immediately done. You have shown me who you are. To be clear...... what do I feel you have shown me? You have shown me you don't respect me or my time. That YOUR time is important. But mine isn't. Well, that's an interesting way to attempt to start or continue a relationship by telling the other person that the only things that matter are the ones that affect YOU.

"But Eric, I'm just late... that's just who I am. I'm habitually late. It's part of my DNA..." No... it's not. You are making a choice.

If I told you that if you were early for a meeting at 8 a.m. and when you show up early, you will be rewarded with two million dollars, my guess is that you would figure out a way to be on time. You'd leave earlier than usual. You wouldn't risk traffic making you late. You'd get up earlier to make sure you get everything done at home in time to leave at the appropriate time and secure that two million.

Maybe you're a billionaire, and two million doesn't mean anything to you. But there is a number. And regardless of what that number is, I bet I'm right. What that says is this: it IS possible to always be early or on time. YOU just aren't willing to make the sacrifices necessary to make it happen. Because, really—who gives a shit, right? I'll tell you who does. The person sitting across from you. You don't like being judged? Then stop giving people opportunities to do it. And I'll tell ya right now—if you pull that kind of shit with me, I'm judging you.

Lastly, and this couldn't be simpler, if you HAVE to be late. CALL. Don't be an asshole.

These little things start to add up. Don't promise something if you're going to blow it off. People are watching you.

You might think, *Ah, it's just a small little thing.* But all these small little things add up to an extremely large thing. You're either building trust, or you're destroying it. What do you do on a daily basis with the people in your life? Really think about it. Take an inventory of each person you interact with on the regular. You might be surprised who you take for granted. Don't do that. Those are the ones you can't afford to lose. The people we take for granted are the ones we usually need the most. This goes for our "right-hand guys" at the office and our partners at home. Make sure they are getting trust investments as much or more than everyone else around you.

One small action at a time. So, you have a choice as you're doing things. Every decision you make is, obviously, a choice—and it's a choice of building trust or destroying it.

I want you to ask yourself a couple of questions while you're reading this book. How many times have you made promises to people? How many times have you broken those promises? And if you did break a promise, what happened in that relationship? And when you broke that promise, what did you do next? What you do next is always the most important thing. What I do next is take an inventory of where I was wrong. I stole this from the steps of AA, but it holds true for everyone. Take an inventory of where you may have wronged someone and promptly admit it. If you make a mistake, own up to it. Make the apology. Right the wrong. Then, you're able to move on. Don't let it sit there and fester—because it WILL fester. It will grow and make it much harder to fix down the line.

The question is: *Why is trust essential?* It's essential because if people don't trust you, they're not going to follow you. If they don't follow you, you won't be able to get the results you're looking for in your business or your life.

Why would ANYONE actually follow you if they didn't trust you? They might "hang around" for a little while, but once they realize you don't do what you say... they're gone. No one wants to be around that kind of person for the long term, no matter how much money you pay them. Well, maybe you can get them to stick around longer if you overpay them (lol)—but not long term.

What does trust look like as a leader? If I tell somebody who works for me that I'm going to meet with them to go over KPIs and have a review with them, and then I cancel it, it might make them think that whatever else I'm doing is more important than that. It tells them subconsciously that I don't care about them. Now, this is probably not the case, but you just took a withdrawal from the person's "trust bank."

Every time we do something, we're either adding to that trust bank or we're taking away from it. We've all heard this concept from Stephen Covey, author of *The 7 Habits of Highly Effective People,* but if you haven't, the idea is that you continually make "trust deposits" with your people. The more deposits that you make—like with a bank account—the less your account will be impacted when you make a withdrawal.

So, how do you use this in your business and your life? If you've made three hundred trust deposits and have to cancel a meeting, it isn't going to be super significant to that person because your trust account has been built up so high. But if you've only made five trust deposits and take one out, the account kind of feels that sting, right? If you have five dollars and somebody asks for two, it's a big deal. If you have a million dollars and somebody asks for two, it's not really that big of a deal.

Imagine trying to make a withdrawal when you haven't made any deposits. Now you're negative. You can't make withdrawals if your account's negative. This is why it's so important to gain trust and make

7

these trust deposits. You have to make daily deposits to build up that account. You have to be interested in people. You have to ask questions and engage in conversation about what excites them. Do them favors. If someone asks you for a favor, do whatever you can to grant it. Nothing builds trust more than favors or helping somebody with something. Don't sacrifice what you're doing and what's important just to grant a favor (obviously) but doing a favor for someone or helping someone when it stings a little?... Gamechanger. Try it.

I want to dig into this a little more: doing favors for people. Have you ever had someone do you a favor? Think about it... How did that make you feel? You probably had an overwhelming feeling of appreciation, right? If that person asked you for a favor down the road, you would be pretty hesitant to say no, wouldn't you? Because you would feel like you "owed" them or because you like to do things for good people? Ah... which one is it? Is it a little of both? Yeah, that's what it is for me, too. I like to say that I'm altruistic and that it's just because I help good people, but let's be real. It's both. You get to feel good. They appreciate it, AND you got one in the bank.

Now if you're the type of person who holds that shit over someone's head, you're an asshole. Don't do that... but business is built on favors. Business is built on relationships and helping people out. And guess what? When it's time for the big contract, they remember. "Oh, yeah... remember when Eric did that shit for me? Yeah. We should give that contract to Eric, for sure." So, the moral of the story is... do favors—as many as you can afford to and even when you can't. Let me tell you, it comes back in spades.

Now, I'm going to reiterate this: Do what you say you're going to do. Show up when you say you're going to show up. If you can't show up, tell them. If you need more than fifteen minutes, tell them that. Every time you go back on what you said you would do, you're making withdrawals from that trust account, and you need to be extremely intentional about keeping your balance in the black. There is nothing harder to do than get out of the hole. We all know how hard it is to get out of a financial hole. It is significantly harder to get out of an emotional or trust hole. Anyone who has been married or in a relationship should be able to attest to that.

The last thing that I want to say about trust is that it equals safety. When people feel safe, it allows them to trust you. People feel safe because they know that you're going to do the things that you said you're going to do. So, to be the leaders that we are striving to be, we have to consistently make people feel safe in their environment. Ask yourself, *What am I doing in my world to make them feel safe?*

Each person might need something different. One person might need money to feel safe. Another might need to know that someone is there to listen to them. Someone else might need to know that there is no ceiling to their earning potential. There are so many things... but feeling safe is universal. Find out what makes each person feel that way. Ask them, "What do you need to feel safe and in control of your destiny?" Then, let them talk. See what they say and then incorporate that into your world, life, and business.

Now, I want to give you a challenge to work on your trust. This is called the intentional listening challenge, and it focuses on being fully present in conversations and showing people that they're valued by listening attentively and responding thoughtfully.

First, I need you to think of a person whom you interact with regularly; it could be a family member, partner, colleague, or friend. Ideally, you want to choose someone with whom there's room for a deeper connection or who you sense might feel unheard at times.

Next, you're going to plan a time to sit down to have a one-on-one conversation with this person. It doesn't have to be formal, just a natural chance to catch up, but you're still going to plan it. Your goal is to focus completely on them, asking about their interests, their challenges, or any recent experiences they might've had. Try to make the conversation entirely about that. I want you to use open-ended questions that allow that person to share more, such as "How have things been going for you lately?" or "What's something that you're excited about right now?" That's a really good one, by the way. People love talking about what they're excited about, what they're passionate about.

Reflect on what they said, and then repeat it back to them in your own words to show that you're paying attention: "So, you're saying you're excited about the new project but a little bit worried about the deadlines, right?" Limit your responses, though. Let them talk. Focus on asking questions or affirming what they're saying rather than jumping in with your own thoughts or advice. This isn't about you. This is about them.

Then you're going to follow up. After the conversation, identify something that they were passionate about and follow up to see how it is going.

That will show them that you actually remembered what they were talking about, which means that you were listening. This will build trust.

When you get done with this, I want you to reflect on the experience and pay attention to any changes in how they now respond to you or open up to you without prompting. When you show them that you care about their experiences, you'll likely see them reciprocate that attention and openness.

> **Use the worksheet on the "free stuff" link to help you and your team utilize this exercise.**
>
> **OR SCAN THE QR CODE:**

TWO

BE PRESENT, SHUT THE F*CK UP, AND LISTEN

"When people talk, listen completely. Most people never listen."
– Ernest Hemingway

have a daughter, and her name is Teegan, with two E's, like a golf tee. Yes, that was planned. When we were getting ready to have our daughter, my goal was that one day, she would be on the leaderboard in a golf tournament. When we decided that her name would be Teegan, my wife asked me, "How do you want to spell it?"

I specifically said, "With two E's, like a golf tee, so that when she's on the leaderboard, everybody will look and go, 'Well, that was really well thought out.'" Now, when she introduces herself to people, she literally says, "My name is Teegan with two E's, like a golf tee."

Something else that was planned was her birthday. Teegan was due on May 25th, 2015. Turned out I had a golf tournament that weekend. So, we went into the OB's office for a follow-up, and I thought I'd ask a question. "Hey, Doc... so, here's the thing. I have a golf thing on the twenty-fifth. What are your thoughts on shitting this kid out a week early? My birthday is May eighteenth. Let's induce on the seventeenth and give her my b-day. I'm old. I don't need a b-day. I want to give it to her. I want to have that connection for the rest of my life and hers, even when I'm gone. Oh, and even when she's a teenager and wants to yell at me, she still has to deal with the fact we have the same birthday."

She's nine now, and let me tell you... I never thought I'd love having Barbie and Elsa cakes for my birthday. But I absolutely love it. I don't know if anything makes me happier than sharing that day with her. The day I turned thirty-six, my wife gave me the most amazing birthday present I could ever been given. Teegan. (I love you, baby!)

When Teegan was about three, we started going to have ice cream every Sunday. It was just kind of on a whim. I thought, *Oh, this will be cool. Let's just go have ice cream. Kids like ice cream.* One Sunday became the next Sunday and the next Sunday, and I started to realize what it meant to be present, what it meant to just be there for her, and what it meant to start making memories. So, we started documenting it.

Every Sunday, we started taking pictures and videos of us eating ice cream and posting them on social media to let everybody know that we were taking that time to be together no matter what because I travel a lot for work.

I'm on the road a decent amount, whether I'm at speaking engagements, filming podcasts, or dealing with my regular business in the roofing space. What I've come to learn is that it's not about the quantity of time we spend together; it's about the quality of the time. It's about what we're doing with the time that we have. My daughter is not going to remember if I sat around the house watching TV for three weeks in a row and I was just there, existing. I could be there for a month straight and do nothing and make no memories, and she is not going to grow up and remember those times. She's going to remember the times that we were intentional about being together.

So, that was why we started documenting it. I knew that I wasn't the only one who was fearful about falling into the trap of quantity over quality, and I wanted other people to see that they could make a difference in their kids' lives by showing up and making sure that they were present at that moment.

It got to a point where I'd go to conferences and take Teegan with me, and people would walk up to her and say, "You're the ice cream girl, aren't you?" We started doing that when she was three years old. As of the writing of this book, she is currently nine, so we've been doing it for almost six years now.

If you do the math, six years times fifty-two weeks is three hundred twelve Sundays. Due to travel or work, I have missed about eight Sundays, which is not very many. But let me tell you, she knows that I've missed eight because sometimes I'll say, "I haven't missed many of these, honey. I make sure that I'm always here," and she'll reply, "Dad, you've missed eight."

Jesus, girl... eight out of three hundred twelve? She's rough.

She knows every single one that I've missed. Why? Because they are that important to her. Think about that. That one day is so important that she can remember the eight that I missed. We became so famous at the local Dairy Queen that they actually made us t-shirts to thank us for coming in and using their space to be able to be present.

The reason that the title of this chapter is "Be Present, Shut the F*ck Up, and Listen" is because the world has turned into an extremely noisy place. We're not taking the time to actually listen to other people. We're not being present in the moment and listening to what other people are saying. We need to give meaning to those moments.

We give meaning by connecting—and by the time you get done reading this book, all of this will have come together. What we're trying to do at the end of the day is find a connection with people. Whether these people are in our businesses or our homes, we're looking to find connections. So, we need to be present in the moment.

I don't believe in balance. I believe in being one hundred percent invested in the thing that you're doing in the moment that you're doing it. If you do that, you will end up finding the "balance" that you're looking for. For the record... balance... is... bullshit. It's not a thing. By its very definition, it screams "mediocre." Balance makes me think of a teeter-totter from when I was a kid: When you are both sitting there halfway up in the air, and it's not moving... balance. Cool. Nothing. Is. Happening. You're just sitting there. We gotta make shit happen. So, slam that damn thing into the ground. Shoot your buddy to the sky. Then do it yourself. Keep moving, but focus on where your feet are when you are on that teeter-totter. Pay attention. Don't be the asshole blowing dandelions in the outfield. Be present.

If I'm not present at work because of distractions that might be going on at home, when I do finally go home, I'm going to have that world infiltrating my life there. That isn't going to allow me to be present with the people I need to be present with—and the same thing goes at work.

13

When we're at work, when we're having meetings, when we're sitting in front of our computer, when we're doing whatever it is that's important at that moment, if we're thinking about something that's going on at home, we're not going to be able to accomplish the goals that we're striving toward. Now we're not one hundred percent invested in what we're doing at work, which means that when we finally go home, we're not going to be fully invested in what we're trying to accomplish there, including spending time with people, and then nothing's going to get done.

So, where's the balance that you're looking for? How do you find it? You have to set standards and expectations with your office team and your family. You have to set boundaries to have balance. My family knows that when I'm at work, I'm at work. Unless the house is burning down and there's something that I can do to actually help put it out, they are not going to bother me during that time.

I set a boundary with my wife when we first started dating. When I met her, we had dinner, and I said, "Look, here's the deal with me. I'm sober. I don't drink anymore. I don't go out and party with the guys. I don't hang out at the bar all night. I'll always be home for dinner.

"But what I do like to do is golf. I love golfing a lot. When I go golfing, though, that's what I'm doing. And I can't be distracted when I'm golfing because I won't play very well, and then I won't be able to enjoy it. I'll come home unhappy because I didn't play very well and didn't have any fun, even though that was meant to be my four hours to disconnect and have a good time.

"So, the boundary is don't call me when I'm golfing. Don't text me when I'm golfing. My phone will be on 'do not disturb,' and I won't answer. But as soon as I'm done golfing—again, I won't be hanging out at the bar. I won't be hanging out at the golf course. I'll be coming home."

We have to do the same thing at work, telling our people, "When I go home, I'm at home, and everything can wait until the next day." There is almost nothing that can't wait until the next day. If we set those same expectations and boundaries with our people at home, it will give us the opportunity to be present while we're at work.

The people we are leading need us just as much from us as the people at home. They're looking at us to show them the way. They're looking at us to make sure that they become successful. And if we are being distracted by something else when we are supposed to be leading them and helping them, what exactly are they supposed to think? If it were me, I would think that my boss or leader didn't think I was important. I would think that they didn't really care about my success or what happened to me. Now, that probably couldn't be further from the truth, but perception is reality. Remember that. It is hard to change a perception if you don't do things the right way.

Our people are looking at us to make sure that they're doing their job right and making the right decisions. And if we're not one hundred percent invested in doing that while we're there, being present, then nothing is going to be accomplished. We're not going to reach the goals that we want to reach as an organization.

The people we lead aren't going to reach their goals because they're always going to be thinking that something else is more important. We can't bleed through. Being present also means asking questions and then shutting the f*ck up and listening.

What do you need from me to be able to help you? And then, once you ask that question, shut the f*ck up. Let them answer. Let them tell you what they need. Let them tell you how you can help them. Everybody always wants to interrupt and be the smartest guy in the room. If you're the smartest guy in the room, as the old adage says, you need to find a new f*cking room.

You don't know everything. If you're self-aware enough to know that you don't know everything, you're going to be successful. But when people walk into a room with an ego, and they're worried about what people think of them and if they're going to have the right answer, there's no opportunity to learn.

First of all, nobody wants to work with or for somebody who always has to be that guy. No one wants to work and be around somebody who has to always one-up everyone else. We all know that guy, right? We say something like, "I caught a fish this big," and they immediately reply, "Oh, that's great. Would you believe that I caught one this much bigger?" Shut the f*ck up.

Don't be the one-up guy. You don't have to know everything. Be a student.

Walk into every room with a student mindset. If you can treat every meeting as an opportunity to learn something and not just as an opportunity to teach someone something, you are going to selfishly gain so much information. But then, what you do with that information is what matters.

What are you going to do with that information that people give you when you are quiet and present? You will be able to solve people's problems when you actively listen to their answers.

Again, I've been in recovery and sober since 2010. I've attended twelve-step meetings for fifteen years—longer than that, actually, because I got in trouble many, many times. We'll get to those stories later.

But when people go to AA meetings, a lot of them sit there and listen to others speak. Actually, I should rephrase that: They hear words come out of other people's mouths. Many times, though, what they're really doing—and ask yourself if you've ever done this before—is trying to figure out what they're going to say when the person stops talking. They're just literally waiting in the wings for their turn to speak.

They're waiting to one-up, to tell their story, but they're not actually listening to the other person. They're not being present at that moment. Be present when people are speaking to you. If you really listen, you might learn something. But when we close our minds off to thinking someone else might have a point of view we haven't heard and could learn from, we close ourselves off to growth.

Be present when you're outside, sitting at the lake, watching an amazing, beautiful sunset. Be present when you're on vacation with your family and are on a boat in the middle of the ocean. Be present in those moments to absorb that feeling of just being and having that experience that you're having because you're never going to have that same experience with those same people ever again.

At every mastermind retreat that I attend or that I put together, I remind everybody that this moment we're having at this dinner table or on this boat—because we go scuba diving on all of our mastermind retreats—with this exact group of people is never going to happen again. So, you need to take the time right now to appreciate it.

You need to take the time to own what it is that you're going through right now. Appreciate and love this moment that you're sitting in, good or bad. As the saying goes, "This, too, shall pass." We always associate that with when "bad" things are happening to us, but guess what? When shit is good, "This, too, shall pass." It all will. It's a never-ending cycle, so just accept that and then be in THAT moment.

Be present in it. Sit in it. Be quiet. Meditate. Hear the moment. Feel the moment. Feel the wind, smell the smells, and hear the sounds. Be present in that moment so you can remember it—not so that you can recreate it but so that you can appreciate it because that moment will never happen again.

Something else this reminds me of is about being present with those we care about who might not have much time left. Don't take those people for granted in your life. We're not going to live forever.

As much as I am trying to figure out a way to live forever and make my daughter freeze in time so that she never gets older than nine, I haven't done it yet—but God damn it, I am trying. One day, we won't be here. One day, the people we care about and are with right now won't be here. And let me tell you, that still scares the shit out of me. Everyone who writes a book always seems so well adjusted and seems to have their spiritual journey "figured out." I say, "F*ck those guys!" Lol. I am still scared of death. Actually, I'm scared of not being there for the people who need me. I am not egotistical enough to think that they will need me forever, but... shit... I kind of want them to. I like to be needed. Don't you? So, to all the fake gurus out there pretending death isn't scary, f*ck off. It is.

One of my biggest regrets is not spending enough time with my grandfather. Now, that being said, I did spend a lot of time with him. I lived with my grandfather from when I was seven years old until I went to college. For all intents and purposes, he raised me. He was my dad. He took me to get my hair cut, and I had my first drink with him. We went to the horse track together.

Before he died, I got to take him to the Kentucky Derby. That was always his dream. We got to watch a Triple Crown winner win the first leg. He took me to the local track in the neighborhood of Aksarben in Omaha. Let's talk about how creative that name is. The track was in Omaha, Nebraska. Now spell Aksarben backwards... Got it? Anyway I have SO many amazing memories with my grandfather at that horse track. He taught me how to read the program when I was ten. I knew all the jockeys. I knew all the trainers. I knew you don't bet a horse; you bet a jockey or a trainer because good jockeys and good trainers don't ride shitty horses.

Okay, sorry, I have a story about going to the track with my Gramp. Gramp would let me bet on a horse when I was very young—like seven or eight. I would read the program and tell him who I wanted. He would go get me the ticket. He taught me you don't make the stupid exotic bets like exacta and trifectas. You bet on a horse either to win and place or across the board if the odds are good enough. "Across the board" means win, place, and show (first, second, or third).

The first race of the day was generally a maiden race, meaning all the horses were "maidens"—they've never won a race. Usually, the favorite is a horse that has placed in the top three multiple times but just hasn't broken into the winner's circle. Well, I was eight or so, so clearly, I knew what I was doing. I told Gramp I wanted two dollars across the board on a horse that had NEVER run a race. EVER. I'll never forget that horse's name: "Little Irish Nut."

So, Gramp goes and bets his horse. Tells me he's got my ticket, and we go outside to watch the race. Race starts, and Little Irish Nut jumps out to the front, fast... *Shit*... That usually isn't good. Why? Well, normally, they blow through all their energy, and by the time they get to the home stretch, they run out of gas, and a horse that has been pacing properly will catch them and overtake them in the end.

Well, this Little *f*cking* Irish Nut just keeps going. He opened up leading by three lengths. Then five. By the time he crossed the finish line, he had won that race by almost ten lengths. Just flying! I was so happy. Jumping up and down, losing my mind. I looked at my Gramp, and his head was staring straight down at the floor.

Now, what I forgot to tell you is that this horse was a long shot. He was like 89-1. That means if you bet a dollar, you'd win eighty-nine dollars if he won. Gramp decided he wasn't going to waste his own six dollars betting that POS long-shot horse for his eight-year-old grandson. He'd just book the bet himself. Well, I won. That ticket paid well over five hundred dollars across the board.

And here's the lesson: my Gramp did exactly what he said he was going to do. He paid me—out of his own pocket. Never questioned it. Because that's what he said he was going to do.

I never realized how important that lesson was to me until later in life. Thanks, Gramp.

Me and Gramp at the Kentucky Derby - 2014

We made some amazing memories together, and we also worked together. He started our business, D&M Roofing, back in the '60s, and I am now the president and CEO. I carry on his name and legacy the best that I can.

Everything that I do is to make him proud. And I was with him all the time—I mean, all the time—yet my biggest regret is still not spending more time with him. Not appreciating those moments that we had together. Not asking more questions.

God, I wish I could go back and ask more questions to understand who he was when he was my age. I never thought to ask that.

I never thought to ask what mistakes he made in the business when he was my age. I never thought to ask him what mistakes he made with my grandma. I never thought to ask him what mistakes he might've made raising his kids, raising my mom, raising my aunt and uncle.

What things would he have changed when we came to live with him? Then he passed away. I've had to guess from what I saw and what I remember, and I wish that those moments had been burned into my brain.

I wish I had old VHS tapes of him telling me stories. It's so weird how you can start to forget what somebody you were so close to looked like. I wish I had been more present, and I wish I had really listened.

I wish I would have shut the f*ck up and listened more. When my grandpa was on his deathbed, he hadn't spoken in a couple of days. He was out of it and hadn't opened his eyes.

His dream before that was to be able to watch Teegan grow up. He kept saying, "I just want to be around long enough to watch her walk," and in the back of my head, I'd think, *Whew. That's going to be a tough one, Gramp.*

They had a month together. She was born on May 18, 2015. My grandfather passed away in June 2015. He wanted to spend every moment with her, to be present. It might've taken him eighty years to really learn what it meant to be present.

He knew that he wanted to be present with her, and I wanted nothing more than for him to have that. And it was taken away so fast.

As he lay on his deathbed—and hadn't opened his eyes in a couple of days—I had a picture of Teegan on the screen of my phone. For whatever reason, I walked up to him and held the phone up to his face. I said, "Hey, Gramp, do you know who this is?"

He actually opened his eyes. Then he looked at the photo, lifted his fragile little hand, pointed at it, and said, "I love her."

Then his hand dropped, and he closed his eyes. And that was the last time that he said anything. That was the last time that he opened his eyes.

Twenty-four hours later, I was in the room with him and one other person, with my hand on his heart so that I could actually feel his last breath when he passed away. It got taken away so fast, his opportunity to be present with Teegan and her opportunity to be present with him.

Writing this right now makes me well up a little. But he got some time. Teegan got some time. Not enough, but some.

What do we do with the amount of time that we have? What are you doing with that time? Do you waste it and just exist in a room with your family, with your people at work? Or are you intentional about being in that moment? If you don't get anything else out of this book, I want you to be intentional, to be present with your people, and to shut the f*ck up and listen to what they're saying.

Ask questions, and then shut up. Ask more questions, and then shut up. This will change your life.

The point here is that we want to build more trust and develop more connections. We want to gain knowledge and memories.

Don't just wait to speak. Be present with the people you care about and the people you lead.

Don't show up to a meeting and just exist. Participate, listen, help, and do favors.

I want to challenge you to do something. Schedule a time with someone important to you. Then, go into that time with them with the intention of serving them and being present.

You're going to ask them questions and not expect anything in return. You're going to sit through an entire conversation with this person and not talk about yourself at all. You're not even going to give an example of how you can relate to their story. You're just going to let them talk. Then you're going to ask them more questions.

Learn more about your people to build on that foundation of trust by being present, shutting the f*ck up, and listening.

THREE
EMPATHY

*"Empathy is simply listening, holding space, withholding judgment,
emotionally connecting, and communicating that
incredibly healing message of 'You're not alone.'"*
– Brené Brown

The second pillar of the T.E.A.M. Method is *empathy*.

I want to start with a story from about five years ago. This is when I learned a special way to interact and connect with some people thanks to someone that I now have the pleasure of calling a good friend. His name is Sam Taggart, and I met him a while back at this conference.

Sam was this long-haired Mormon kid from Utah, and we had nothing in common. He ran a door-to-door consulting business. He looked like a hippie but was Mormon as shit. I'm pretty sure that he was still wearing his garments underneath his clothes. I mean, we had nothing in common. I was an old, recovering alcoholic pile of shit, and he was this kid whom, I assumed, nothing bad had ever happened to in his life. For whatever reason, though, we hit it off.

I just kind of left it at that. Then, a month or so later, Sam reached out to me and asked me to join his mastermind group. *Why?* I wondered. *Why would I join a group with this guy?* Again, we had nothing in common. He then told me that I needed to book a flight and come meet him and his group in Mexico in a week.

I just started laughing at him. "You're out of your mind," I said. I was not going to book a flight to go hang out with what I thought at the time was just a bunch of Mormon kids in Mexico. But then I started thinking about it, and I was like, *Okay, I need to get out of my comfort zone. I need to do some shit that makes me uncomfortable.*

So, I talked to my wife. "Should I go on this trip?" I asked her.

"You love going on trips," she answered. "If you want to do it, do it."

So, I did it. I booked a flight and went on a trip that completely changed my life. This trip was the catalyst for me to grow into the human that I am today. I learned things about myself that I never knew before.

We had to sit next to a river for twelve hours with no food. All we had was a ten-by-ten-foot area, a notebook, a jug of water, and a chair—and it was one of those little fold-up chairs, the kind you take to watch your kids play soccer. They would leave you there and then walk two hundred yards down the river to meet the next person. So, you couldn't see anybody else or even holler at them. You couldn't do anything except sit there.

So, I set my chair down and took a seat in it. Immediately, the f*cking chair breaks.

Now I'm sitting next to a river for the next twelve hours and can't talk to anybody. All I can do is stare at the sun and write with no f*cking chair and a rock to lean on.

Oh, I lied. I also had a towel that I could lay my head on.

All I had to do all day was journal. Every now and then, I'd stare at the sun and try to figure out what time it was. I knew that at nine o'clock, they were going to come back and pick us up so we could return to the house.

I felt like f*cking Davy Crockett or some other person from the old west, staring at the sun, trying to figure out what time it was: "Is it one o'clock? Is it two o'clock?" I don't know who the f*ck I thought I was.

I also fell in and out of sleep. I would nod off for thirty minutes and then wake up, and then I'd start journaling again, writing down things that I wanted to do in my life.

Over the next three years, I did all of those things and had to start making a new list.

A couple of years later, I got to go on another trip with Sam. This time, we went to a place called Lake Powell, and I lived on a houseboat with fifteen other dudes. Now, most of these guys were from a different upbringing than me. Sam attracted a lot of Mormon kids from Utah. Most were very religious.

I am not very religious. Actually, I should rephrase that. I am not religious at all.

I consider myself very spiritual. I thank my God for AA and for helping me find my own higher power, but I'm very anti-religious. I'll state that now.

This is my book. I can say whatever the f*ck I want. I don't support organized religions. I don't support organizations that judge someone and publicly or privately condemn them to a mythical place of fire and brimstone if they don't believe in their God. I don't believe a newborn child that wasn't born into your "religion" on the other side of the world is doomed because you haven't had a chance to fill him/her in on how YOUR GOD is the TRUE GOD. Get f*cked.

To be clear to everyone right now reading this and getting extremely butt-hurt and upset. I support YOU and YOUR ability to pray, worship, and believe in ANYTHING you wish. Whatever you choose to believe in that makes you OK, I 100% support it. For YOU. But not for everyone. I don't support the mindset that because of what you believe, anyone that disagrees is wrong. Because again, it's a BELIEF. And beliefs are great to have. I just don't and won't support people and organizations that package their beliefs as FACTS.

Yes, I realize this statement is going to piss some people off, and some might want to stop reading right now. I challenge you not to give in to that temptation. This is just my opinion. It serves me. I don't expect it to serve everyone. I respect everyone's right to believe in WHATEVER they want. But just remember something. It is a belief. NOT A FACT.

This is the reason I have the disdain I have for most organized religions. Because most of them don't see it that way—they see it as ACTUAL TRUTH. Which implies facts are attached to that truth. If you don't believe what they believe, then you are damned to hell or whatever. *Eh...* that's bullshit (my opinion again, lol).

I believe in doing the next right thing. I believe if you live by that mantra, then whatever happens, happens. I'll accept the consequences.

Sorry, back to the story...

So, like an asshole, I went in with preconceived judgments about these people. I knew that the word "f*ck" alone would make all of them very uncomfortable. Because of that, I was one hundred percent myself on this trip, good and bad. I wanted to find out if they could handle my shit. I told all my stories about being in jail, selling drugs, being a drunk and an addict, all of them.

At the end of the trip, we had to do this exercise. I should rephrase that. We GOT to do an exercise. You always get to do everything in life. You don't have to. But we got to do this exercise. It was called a feedback circle, and each of us had to stand in front of the group and be open to feedback.

You had to stand there like an asshole with your arms open up, facing the person talking to you so that you could accept the feedback. My first reaction was, *This is some hippie shit that I do not want to be involved in.*

However, I had to be open to accepting the feedback, so I said, "I accept your feedback." I didn't really accept their feedback, though.

During this feedback, one gentleman who didn't know me at all told me that I needed to change how I spoke. Apparently, I had offended his sensitive baby ears. I said out loud, "I accept your feedback with my arms open," like a hippie.

On the inside, though, I was like, *You can go f*ck your feedback. Who the hell are these twenty-five-year-old assholes to tell me how I needed to change, how I needed to speak, and how I needed to communicate?* For the rest of the trip, I was pissed off and planned on quitting this group.

The following day, we had to take the boat back, and I rode in the ski boat with Sam back to the dock. He was asking me what I thought of the trip. How did it go? Was I going to rejoin the group? Any advice that I could give for next time? Honestly, I kept pushing off the questions. I kept steering the conversation in a different direction. Finally, we got back to the dock, and I decided that I was going to tell him exactly what I thought.

I was going to give him a piece of my mind.

I told him that I didn't appreciate the feedback. I was actually pretty upset and hurt by it.

At the time, Sam was a very committed Mormon, so I expected him to agree with the feedback I was given. He didn't. He told me that I didn't need to buy into that. He told me that I needed to double down on who I really was and that the people who responded to that were the ones that I should be concerned about.

Comedian Sam Kinison summed this up best when he said that it's not about everyone liking you; it's about a small percentage of the planet that f*cking love you. When you truly understand that, it will change your world. Life will become so simple, and you'll be free.

The point of that story is that I spent all that time assuming that I was going to be judged, and then I was. However, when I went to the person who facilitated what I thought was the judging and told him about it, he looked at me and said, "No, man. Be you." It was the most empathetic moment that I've ever shared with another man. Because of that moment, we became so much closer, and I will follow him anywhere.

And I have. I've gone on numerous additional trips with Sam. He broke my arm. He almost got me killed on Lake Powell again, stranded in the desert with no boat because it floated away.

However, because of that one moment of empathy, of true, genuine empathy, I will follow him wherever he asks me to go. I know that we have a connection through shared experience, and I realize that he genuinely gives a shit about me and my well-being.

Why is this important? Because today, we are not programmed to be empathetic. Social media, the regular media—all the media—are programming us to become so ingrained in our thought processes and belief systems that we have no opportunity to actually listen to other people.

Now, empathy is the ability to understand and share the feelings of another person. Understanding the feelings of other people can be extremely difficult. Why? Because we're usually so wrapped up in our own shit, in our own lives, that we don't want to take the time to actually listen to someone else. Who wants to think that they might be wrong about something?

Here's a little advice.

Sometimes, you are f*cking wrong. Sometimes, it's worth it to open your mind and listen to someone else's point of view. You might be able to learn something from them and their life experience that you can't see through your own lens.

Why does this make a difference? Because it's not common practice. People always ask, "What makes your company different? How do you stand out from the competition?" You always have to find that one thing that other companies don't do. It's the same thing with showing empathy. It's not widely done, right? You have to be different. You have to learn to be empathetic and understand other points of view even when you don't agree, especially when you don't agree.

So, what does empathy mean in business? When you can see the customer's point of view, we all know that makes you the most powerful person in the room. The person who can only see their own point of view is always handicapped because no one else cares about what *you* want.

They care about what *they* care about. You already do that with customers to get their business. Or you should be. What you need to do now is transfer that and do it with your employees so you keep them for years to come.

How can you level up your empathy? Having empathy is one of the most powerful tools you can use to connect with people. I have very strong opinions on lots of issues, but here's something else I have a very strong belief in: Most people are coming from a good place, even if misguided or misinformed, even if I think they are delusional and completely way off base.

Because of that, I want to learn more about them and find out why they have the viewpoints that they do. I want to find out what makes them tick and what events have happened in their lives to make them that way. That shit is interesting to me. Is it interesting to you? Do you actually care about other people and how they see things? Or are you so wrapped up in your own shit that you don't even think about it?

I'll give an example of that. I had the honor and privilege of working with a certain person over the last few years, and we became extremely close. We traveled together and got to know each other really well, but we couldn't have come from more different worlds.

She lived in a different world than me, with different viewpoints on a lot of things. I'm a jock, hunter, gun owner, loud, independent, libertarian —overall, probably pretty obnoxious. She's a gay, quiet, skater, Democrat, and one of the most caring people you could hope to meet. But we would sit together and talk, and I would get an understanding of what she had gone through in her life to become the person she is today and have the beliefs that she does. She would listen to me talk about the things that I went through that shaped me and gave me the opinions and viewpoints that I have.

Neither of us judged the other. We just listened to each other. I never told her why she was wrong, and she never told me why I was wrong. No one wants to be around someone who's always right. I don't want to discuss topics when I know the person is so close-minded that they won't listen to anything that anyone else has to say.

I consider this person a true friend. We would do anything for each other, even though we probably don't vote for the same person or pray to the same God. Isn't that crazy?!—that we can love people who don't agree with us?

It's the same thing with our employees. We want them to follow us for years, not weeks. We want connections and long-lasting relationships.

The whole point here is not to lose people and to grow them as humans. Again, this goes back to empathy. The media wants us to be so divided because that makes money. What you have to understand is that there is money in empathy, especially in your business. People are going to perform at a higher level when they feel understood and appreciated. Your ROI is going to go through the roof because people feel heard.

Many of us are focused on the ROI of everything that we do. When it comes to something like empathy, it is often hard to see fiscally what the ROI is, but you have to understand that your ROI is your people. Your ROI is getting your people to a level of performance that they didn't know was possible. That's only going to happen when you're employing empathy and taking time to understand people and where they come from. It is a hard skill to learn, but if you don't have it naturally, you can learn it.

It takes practice. It takes conversations. This goes back to the previous chapter. You have to have a lot of conversations, listen, and understand that you're not always right. You have to drop your ego and understand that other people's points of view are valid.

Now, don't confuse empathy with sympathy. Sympathy is "I feel bad for you because your dog died." You can remember what the pain felt like, and you can sympathize with other people's situations and what they're going through. That is not empathy. Empathy is *genuinely* caring where they're coming from, regardless of whether you agree or not. Empathy is understanding that when somebody's dog dies, they will need some time and space to mourn—and then giving them that time and space because you care about them.

This goes for politics and religion, too. One thing that drives me up a f*cking wall is that no one is empathizing with anyone else when it comes to these two volatile topics. So, let's f*cking get into it, kids. Let's get into it.

I did a podcast recently that was titled "Why I Don't Care About Your Religion" because I don't. You know what I care about? You as a person. I give zero f*cks about who you worship.

Here's the flip side of that. A lot of people will judge me if I don't believe the same thing that they believe. Isn't that crazy? Think about that for a minute. I make a statement that I don't care about your religion. What people hear, because they are programmed to, is "I don't care about YOU." Nope. Pay attention... I care about YOU. I don't care that you believe in something. Because that's all it is—a belief. You might be right. You might be wrong. We don't know. You SAY you know... but you f*cking don't. You are just scared to admit you might be wrong because it will blow up everything you've been told for thirty years. I care about you as a human regardless of any of that. I want what's best for you and for you to become who you are supposed to be. If that means having faith in something that I don't... cool. My job isn't to change your mind. It's to empathize with and care about you.

But those SAME people... when I tell them I have a different viewpoint than them, what's the usual response? "OMG, you're going to hell. OMG, the country is going to die because you voted for such and such." Settle down, Judgy McJudger. F*ck. Maybe you should spend a little more time focusing on your shit and less worrying about mine. If your day is consumed worrying about who I pray to, who I vote for, and how many times I said f*ck today... you have more issues that need to be worked out than I do.

Can you guess what I say to those people? We focus too much on our differences. Politics is the same way. I don't automatically judge you if you're of a different political mindset than me. I might have some questions for you to explain to me why you think I should be taxed more. (For example) Why should I have all my money taken away and given to people who don't want to work? I have very strong opinions about this, but that's not what this book is about. What I do believe is that most people genuinely come from a good place, even if I think that they're misguided.

Even if I think that you're a nutbag because, again, you think that I should pay more taxes and I shouldn't be able to keep my money, at the end of the day, I still think that you're coming from a good place because you believe that you're doing the right thing. So, I want to talk to you about it.

Do you do the same thing? Do you take the time to try to understand where somebody else is coming from, especially when you don't agree with them? Do you break down walls that prevent that higher level of communication and cooperation? You wouldn't go to a foreign country and expect everyone there to convert to your standards and follow your expectations. You would go there and make an effort to understand them. Or would you? This is a good time to ask yourself that question. The answer might surprise you.

You need to get outside of your bubble. Get outside of the little world that you live in, where everybody that you talk to believes the exact same f*cking things. Get outside of that. Get a little uncomfortable. Let people tell you why they think you're wrong. You might learn something. It might change your insight on something. It might give you a leg up in a conversation in a sales meeting or a conversation at home with your people. Open up and have a dialogue. Dialogue is what opens the door to connection.

If you remember, we talked about this briefly in a previous chapter. The ultimate goal of this book is to teach you how to make genuine connections with people, with your people in the office, with your people at home, and build your team. Dialogue is the key to that, as is being empathetic in that dialogue.

Now I'm going to challenge you to do something. Are you willing to get a little bit of a break and be a little bit uncomfortable? Because this is going to be a little uncomfortable. If you've noticed, most of my challenges ask you to talk to somebody. That is often the most uncomfortable thing that you can do.

What I need you to do is pick that one person in your life whom you know you disagree with on one thing. It can be religion. It can be politics. If you want to make it a little bit easier, make it your opinion on a work process. And if you want to make it really easy, start with the personal because you already know that they'll be a little more open to listening to you.

Whatever you choose, ask them to sit down with you for thirty minutes for a conversation. Then, I want you to ask them three questions about the thing that you disagree on:

1. Why do they believe what they do?
2. What in their past led them to this belief?
3. How would they change it and fix the situation?

Here's the kicker. Don't talk. You can only listen.

No feedback. You let them talk and answer those questions and let them be heard. Don't say a thing.

When the conversation is done, say, "Thank you," and go on with the rest of your day.

FOUR
AUTHENTICITY

*"It's not about how many people like you, it's about the small percentage of the planet that **f*cking** love you"*
– Sam Kinison

When I was young, I was "the chubby kid." I never felt like I fit in. I always felt alone and on the outside looking in.

This girl in my seventh-grade class was mean to me all the time. One day, this little shit put a bar of soap under my chair with a note that said, "Please take a shower." Man, all I wanted to do was hide under that chair. But remember, I was the fat kid... I couldn't really hide anywhere. Plus, apparently, I stunk... so they would sniff me out even if I did hide.

Now, I was the stinky fat kid, and I'd never felt so alone and inadequate. I was faced with a choice: What could I do about my situation? What would you have done? Crawl in a corner and hide? Man, that's the easy option. That's really what I wanted to do. I could live in that shit. I could accept the fact that I was the stinky fat kid, and that's all I ever would be. Or I could step up and change my mindset.

What did I do? I started playing football. I started eating right. I started getting in shape. I busted my ass and became an all-conference football player at my high school with that confidence. I started figuring out who I was and who I wanted to be. You know what I didn't want to be? The stinky, fat kid who got picked on and bullied. Sometimes, we have to figure out exactly what we DON'T want to be, so we can figure out who we DO want to be.

Now, look... bullying is wrong—let me preface that prior to this next statement—but the shit that happened to me growing up, the feelings of inadequacy, of not being good enough, pushed me. I didn't want to be that kid. I didn't want to grow up and be that adult. I wanted to learn to be confident. I wanted to be comfortable in my own skin. So, I made changes.

Ask yourself, are you willing to make changes? Are you willing to really look at yourself in the mirror and identify your weaknesses? Are you willing to do uncomfortable things? I decided I was. I was willing to put in the hard work to figure it out. It didn't happen overnight, but slowly, I started to creep out of my shell. I started to gain confidence. You know what gives you confidence? Winning. Playing sports, being competitive, or finding anything that you are passionate about. Whatever it is, find your thing.

This came with friends and girlfriends. By the time we graduated, that gal was begging to come to parties thrown by my friends and me. Needless to say, I'm pretty sure I told her to f*ck off. Actually, I'm sure I said that. Maybe not the most adult thing to do... but I was seventeen. What do you expect?

Fast forward twenty years.

Now I'm twice divorced. I'm a raging alcoholic and a drug addict. I'm three hundred ten pounds, a fat piece of shit... again.

I have no desire to even really live anymore. I have no family of my own, no kids. I feel like I'm old, and I don't see any light at the end of the tunnel.

Now, keep in mind, I was only thirty, but I felt extremely old. I only saw darkness and despair. When I was twenty-nine, I got pulled over for going down a one-way street at four o'clock in the morning. I had been selling drugs all night long and had a significant amount on me for my personal use as well. This would be my fourth offense, felony DUI, and the drug charges would probably be extremely significant. I had multiple "teener" bags in my middle console for sale.

If you're asking, "What's a teener?" Basically, it's a hundred dollars worth of coke, and I had ten of them in my middle console. I was the guy who used to sell cocaine on the honor system. I would literally put the bags of coke in the middle console of my truck, and people would text me and

SHUT THE F*CK UP AND LISTEN (MORE)

say, *"Hey, where are you at?"* I'd tell them, and they'd drive to my truck, open up my middle console, grab a "teener," and throw a hundred dollars into the truck. I had very honest clients, apparently, as they always left the rest of the coke in my middle console. It was crazy when I think about it today, but that's what they did.

I also had one or two eight-balls in my cargo pocket. Yes, I was wearing cargo shorts because, back then, they were extremely cool. I was extremely f*cked up on booze, too.

So, when I got pulled over, I knew I was finished. I'd been there before —three times, actually. This was starting to feel old hat... like this was my life. I'd start to feel good about things, get a little taste of success... and BOOM, f*ck up again. "You drank too much again, Eric. You're going to jail again, Eric. WTF is wrong with you, Eric?"

I failed all the sobriety tests and was asked to get into the cop car. Then, the officer went to search my truck. Shit.

He came back to the car and said, "You want this thousand dollars?"

"What?" I said. "What thousand dollars?" Remember, I was hammered and high as shit.

"I found a thousand dollars in your middle console," the cop said.

Oh, shit. That meant I accidentally sold all my coke. (I didn't say that out loud btw) "I'm going to go to jail for a hot second, right?" I said.

"Yeah," the cop replied, "you're going to jail for a minute."

"Well, then give me that so I can keep it for the commissary." Bullet dodged.

Now, what about the coke in my pocket? Well, he patted me down but somehow did not find it in that cargo pocket. I have no idea how he missed it.

As I was sitting in the cop car, I remembered that I had the drugs in my pocket. I was sitting in the front seat cuz, you know... I'm white and privi-leged. No joke, though—I was in the front seat of a cop car with cocaine in my pocket, trying to figure out how the hell I was going to get rid of it before I got processed, and they took my clothes.

When we got close to the precinct, I said to the officer, "Sir, I have really got to take a piss. I know this is going to take a little while to process me and do all the things. Would you mind if I took a piss before you book me?"

He agreed, and when we got there, he took me into the bathroom. Of course, he stood behind me with the door wide open while I took a leak. I peed and peed, and I kept turning my head and looking at him, looking at him, looking at him.

For a split second, he turned his head away; something happened behind him. At that moment, I grabbed the coke out of my pocket, dumped it in the toilet, and flushed. Bullet number two dodged.

This day was both the worst and the best day of my life. It was time for a new beginning, a new direction in my life. Now, why do I tell this story? Because I wasn't living the life that I was supposed to live. I wasn't living authentically. I was pretending to be someone I wasn't. For one thing, I wanted to "fit in" and have "friends." All the people I hung around with were trainwrecks, too. None of us expected much from one another. Get up… go to work for a while, get drunk, find some blow, close a bar down, have an after-hours party… and then rinse and repeat almost every day.

It's exhausting trying to be someone that you are not. You are back to feeling alone. I had already spent a large portion of my life feeling like that. Why the hell was I doing it again? Why was I allowing myself to live like that? I knew I had choices. I knew I could make different ones. I wasn't being the man I was supposed to be.

We are not born to be piles of shit. We are not born to hurt people. We're not born to make our parents stay up all night long, wondering what happened to us, wondering where we were. We're not born to make spouses cry every day, wondering what we're going to do. I was living somebody else's life. I don't know whose it was, but he could have it back.

It was all based on fear. I was terrified that people would find out who I really was, and I wasn't comfortable in my own skin at all. But I had no idea how to change.

If we want to lead the people in our organizations and at home in our family unit, they have to know that we are truly who we put out into the world. How are we showing up as authentic and genuine?

I really like the word "genuine," even better than "authentic." Authenticity has become so overused in today's world. When I started talking about authenticity, not a lot of people were talking about it. That's why I named my podcast *Be Authentic or Get the F*ck Out*. I wanted people to realize that they needed to show up as exactly who they were.

Stop pretending to be the people you see on social media. You don't have to pretend to be Gary Vee, Ed Mylett, or Jocko… You should learn from them. You should strive to emulate their good qualities. But there is only one of them. There is only one of you. Stop wasting time trying to figure out how to NOT be you. That's stupid. You have so many amazing things you can do and be... but when you try to show the world a version of yourself that isn't real, you're wasting your life and talent.

But as the years have gone by, I've seen people start using the word "authentic" in different contexts, and I've come to realize that you can authentically be an asshole. I think I started to associate "authentic" with people being a version that I agreed with, something or someone that I approved of... but that's not how it works. If you're being authentic to yourself, then f*ck anyone who doesn't like or support you. I truly mean that—get rid of them. They shouldn't be in your life. We do not have enough time on this earth to worry about people who don't align with us. Notice I said "align," not "agree." Big difference. I have a lot of people in my life that I don't agree with, but I can still align with them.

Now, that being said, also make sure that you ARE actually being authentic. Lately, all I see is fake bullshit and people putting on a show. "Pay attention to me! Please! I bought some fake clothes! I bought a car I can't afford, and my kids still live in an apartment I can't afford, either!"

I'm going to clue you in on something. We know. We all know you're full of shit, and we are laughing at you. Well, I am. Other people might feel sorry for you.

Eh... shit... I guess I'm both. I'm laughing, and I feel sorry, but I'm also disgusted. Because that was me. I did that. I wanted people to like me. I went places I shouldn't. I did things that didn't align with who I actually was. I sacrificed good years of my life trying to be someone I wasn't. Man... think about that. That's sad as shit. I used GOOD years of my life pretending to be someone else. Not myself. Because I didn't think ME was good enough.

What I realized was that I was really leaning toward wanting people to be genuine. Now, those two words, "authentic" and "genuine" are obviously extremely similar. But when I hear the word "genuine," to me, it means that you're not only showing up as exactly who you are but you're doing all of those things that we talked about in previous chapters. You're showing up and doing exactly what you said you were going to do. Genuine people are who they say they are. When I think that someone is genuine, I also feel like I can trust them. If you remember, this whole thing starts with trust. People are going to trust genuine and authentic people. They are NOT going to trust fake MFers. Would you? Do you run to people who creep you out? No... of course not. You run away like they have the plague.

I think that "genuine" also means that when you say something, you mean it. You're not a liar. You're not hiding behind a bunch of different masks. And I'm not writing a book about masks. There are a million books out there already about wearing masks, so you can go read them. I'm not smart enough and haven't done enough research on all the science behind all the different masks that people wear. But here's what I do know: We all wear them, and when we start pulling them off and showing up as exactly who we are, people respond to that.

Now, it's okay if you don't know exactly who you are right now. You might be going through some shit like I was. You might be living with drug addiction. You might be living in a state of depression because your business isn't going the way that you want it to right now. You might be having issues at home with your family, your wife, or your kids, and you just don't know how to fix them. So, you show up as someone you're not, to try to fix those things. That rarely goes well. It's just like any kind of lie—you can't keep it going forever. Eventually, you're going to get found out. Your fake version of yourself isn't going to be able to solve those problems, but the real you will.

But you're not really showing up as who you are. You're showing up as who you think people want you to be. It's okay to not know right now, but it's not okay to not continuously try to figure it out. It has taken me a significant amount of time to figure out who I am, and I'm still constantly doing it.

Let's be honest. I still have days when I realize some new shit about myself. Some simple things that I have realized over the years are that I say whatever I want, and I say it however I want to say it. And I'm okay with the consequences that come with this. I speak a certain way.

I say "f*ck" pretty often. It's part of my vocabulary. People judge me, ridicule me, and tell me that I'm not intelligent because I can't use or choose not to use other vocabulary to get my point across. While writing this book, I was told we had to change the title because Amazon or some other book lists wouldn't approve of *Shut the F*ck Up and Listen* because of the "naughty" language. Yeah... I don't care. This is exactly who I am. This is exactly how I speak. I am SOOO okay if it pushes you away from me because then I know I don't have to waste my time with you. I WANT who I am to push people away. Then I can figure out who really belongs in my sphere. I'll tell you right now... someone who tells me to be something different from who I am is not one of those people.

I'm not sure why they're so worried about how I speak because I'm not worried about how they speak. I don't tell them that they need to curse more. I don't tell them that they need to do things differently. Usually, people who do that are extremely insecure, and they don't really know who they are.

Which one are you? Are you one of those assholes who always feels the need to tell other people what they're doing wrong? Are you focusing on other people more than you're focusing on yourself? If you are, I'm going to fill you in on a little secret: That's not going to work out real well for you. You're going to live a life where everything is everybody else's fault. Every time I got pulled over, I was always able to find the "reason" it happened. It was never MY fault. It was the semi that jumped out in front of me. Yes, the semi! I have passed out drunk while driving twice in my life —at eighty-five to ninety miles per hour. When I woke up, I was slamming into the back of a semi. Twice. You read that correctly. Twice. I should be dead.

Do you want to know why this happened? Because I was drunk as shit. Because I drank to oblivion and made a decision and didn't think of the consequences at all. I didn't think of the other people on the road that night. I didn't think of my family. I didn't think of anyone but myself. Self-ish. Piece. Of. Shit.

Today, I try to own everything I do and everything that happens to or for me. It's actually liberating. Now, I don't have to figure out who to blame every time something goes wrong. It's me. I am to blame. I can always do better. So can you. Stop blaming shit on other people and take responsibility for your actions and decisions. And stop wasting time. I don't even like wasting time on my clothes.

I wear the same clothes every day. All of my clothes are purchased from the country club where I play golf. I wear golf clothes every day. If it's warm out, I put on golf shorts and a polo, maybe a vest. And if it's cold out, I have on pants, a golf shirt, and a vest or a jacket.

That's it. I show up to business meetings like that. I speak on stage like that.

Now, keep in mind that just a couple of years ago, I was showing up and speaking on stage in a suit jacket because I felt like I needed to "respect" the stage and respect the person who was putting on the event. Now, while that is true, I also need to respect the fact that they hired me.

They hired me, not a version of me. So, I need to show up as exactly who I am so the people who are watching me speak are like, "Oh, that's him." If they see me in any other situation, they're not going to see me in a suit. I don't feel the need to be loud and flamboyant and look a certain part. Here's the reason: People can sniff out that bullshit from a mile away.

If you feel the need to only show your wins on social media, to pretend that you take flights on private jets or drive a Lamborghini or a Ferrari by renting one for a day and taking a picture of yourself by it, and your only concern is getting your followers up, another secret I'm going to fill you in on is that people f*cking know. People know—and as a general rule, people are not attracted to that.

The whole goal here is that we want to get people to trust us to form connections with them. We are never going to do this if people don't believe we are who we portray ourselves to be. If you let go of that façade, you can be genuine. Then you're going to attract people like yourself.

You have to ask yourself, what is my goal here? Is my goal to attract people who are nothing like me? If that's the case, you need to do some soul-searching and find out why you're trying to attract people who aren't like you. Is it because you're not okay with you? Is it because you know there's some shit you need to work on? If so, maybe you should take the time to work on yourself before you start trying to get these amazing people to be around you.

It's the same thing as when we're young and dating. The harder you try to find that person, the less you're likely to find them. The minute that you accept that it's okay to be alone or that you're okay with yourself and you don't "need somebody" to fill a void for you or make you whole, that's the moment that they show up.

You need to be okay with who you are so you can naturally attract those people into your life. If you're genuinely a piece of shit, you're going to attract other pieces of shit. If you are genuinely kind and a positive person, you're going to attract those people. So, you need to figure out how to become the person you want to attract. You won't make any connections with others if you're not genuine—and in business, no one wants to work for a fake motherf*cker.

You will lose every time you show up as something you're not. No one wants to follow someone like that. No one wants to follow fake because people want to feel safe in their work environments, and the only way that happens is if they believe in the person that they're following.

So, what does that mean? It means we need to genuinely work to become the kind of person we want to be. Sometimes, you have to change your environment. Sometimes, you have to get people out of your life. This one can be a little tough because sometimes that's family.

You might have family members in your life who hold you back. You might have people you genuinely care about and want to see do well, but every time you have a conversation with them, they have extremely negative energy and complain. You try to tell them about your future, your plans, the things that you're building, right? As entrepreneurs, owners, and leaders, we have big f*cking ideas, and a lot of them fail. Some of them don't. But when I talk to somebody who doesn't get that and is constantly questioning me negatively and saying, "Oh, you can't do that; that's f*cking impossible," it makes me double down. It makes me want to say, "F*ck you. Watch me. F*cking watch me."

But if you're not okay with yourself and you're not showing up as exactly who you are or confident in what you're doing, those kinds of people can completely take it out of you. If you hear it enough, even if you are okay with it, even if you are extremely confident, it will start sucking the wind out of you. It will start making you question your decisions.

So, again, I know that it's hard, but you have to take a look at yourself and make a list of all the people in your life whom you associate with on the daily, on the weekly, or on the monthly. Then you need to figure out which ones push you forward, raise you up, and make you better and which ones don't. The ones who don't, they don't get your energy. They don't get your time. They're not moving you in the direction that you need to be moved.

Think about what I said earlier about the people who have to go on social media and show a fake persona. What we have to remember is that people do not relate to boasting and one-upping. How many of us have that friend or acquaintance who's a one-upper? In every conversation that you have, they are just WAITING to speak. Not listening to anything you're saying, just getting ready to WOW the shit out of you.

That Instagram lifestyle is absolutely getting found out, and I couldn't be happier about it. People are starting to finally see that it's all bullshit. People are starting to realize that we relate to vulnerability and losses, not wins. I want to know how you have overcome something, how you have worked hard and persevered, not your other bullshit. I don't care. Sorry. Don't try to impress me.

When I go to conferences, I set up my podcast studio and interview people. At one recent conference, a guy approached me and asked to do an interview. This wasn't the first time—at three other conferences, he'd asked the same thing, and I'd kind of blown him off. He just didn't feel right or like he was aligned with what I was trying to accomplish.

At this event, he came up to me again and said, "Hey, man, do you remember me?"

"Yeah, I remember you," I replied. "What's up?"

"Man," he said, "you need to have me on your show now."

"Oh, I do?"

"Yeah, man. You need to have me on your show."

"Okay," I said. "Why do I need to have you on my show?"

He looked me right in the eye and said, "Because I'm f*cking crushing it."

Ew, f*cking gross, man. Who thinks that a conversation like that is going to get somebody to want to spend time with you? It's not. It's all about you. Why aren't you talking about how excited you are to share some of the things that you've done to help other people grow? Why wouldn't you share some of your defeats, failures, and losses and what you learned from those things to become a better person? The real way to be seen and heard is to share those losses. Share those failures and what you learned from them.

It's not just about sharing losses and failures but about discussing what came from those losses, what came from those failures. Be humble. Nobody wants to hang out with somebody who doesn't have humility.

When you first start going to AA meetings and try to find a sponsor, they tell you that you need to look for somebody who has what you want. Obviously, that is not supposed to mean financially, like, "That guy's rich and has a cool house and a car." It's about finding somebody who has what you want spiritually and emotionally, all the things that will make you a better person. What I learned from watching people in these meetings is that the ones who had the valuable assets, the great jobs, the beautiful wives, and all the things that I wanted all had humility.

Every single one of them had humility. They all realized that they weren't the biggest f*cking deal in the world, that they were there to help other people. That's who you want to be, I think. Maybe you don't. If you don't, and you think that your purpose in life is to just show up and make as much money as you can and f*ck everybody else, this book's not for you. You probably already closed the book at this point.

So, everybody who's still along for the ride here is probably on board with what I'm saying. Show up and learn who you are, and if you don't know, take some time and figure it out. Talk to other people.

If you need therapy, go to therapy. If you need a coach, get a coach. Everybody needs a coach. I have a coach; my coach has a coach, and his coach has a coach. We're all constantly figuring out how to be better and how to make sure that we're showing up as exactly who we are. Be humble.

Now, I was telling a story earlier about when I got pulled over. It was October 2009, and my ass was going to jail. It was the worst day of my life. What I didn't know at that time was that it was going to become the best day of my life because that was the day when I stopped being the person I was and started on the journey of becoming the person I was meant to be.

It still makes me laugh to this day. I ended up going to jail that night, and then I got out and spent a month in rehab, finding out what it really means to give back and help people. Since then, I've had the honor and the privilege of co-founding a nonprofit called Roofers in Recovery, where we raise money and send people in the roofing community to treatment when they need it.

We have recovery meetings twice a week, and we've built a community for people in the roofing and construction space. It's an alpha male industry, and nobody wants to talk about what they're going through, so we made a safe space for them to be able to do that.

We get to help put families back together, which is just like what my grandpa always wanted to do: make families whole. If I had never gotten pulled over that day, I would have been dead or in jail and of no service to anyone. Well, I'm sure there are some people in my past who wouldn't have been disappointed by that. Personally, though—and I believe my family today would agree—it would have been a damn shame.

Now, I'd like you to really think about who it is that you want to show up as and who you want to attract in your life. My challenge to you is to make a list of the top three people you admire. They can be celebrities, people close to you, your parents, your grandparents—anybody who is either in your life or who you wish was in your life.

Next, I want you to write down the traits that you love about them. Do you love how they give back to the community? Do you love how they interact with their kids? Do you love how they seem to have a great marriage? Whatever it is, write down the traits that you love about them. Then you're going to write down how many of those traits you already possess. The leftover ones are the ones that you wish you had and need to work on and acquire so that you can become the person you want to be.

Now, you have some action steps to take when you know you're not living your life authentically and genuinely and showing up as who you're supposed to be. Take the time to sit down and make lists to understand who it is that you need in your life so that you can become the person who deserves to have them.

"Fat Eric" Circa 2008

"New Eric" Circa 2025

FIVE
OVERCOMING ADVERSITY, FACING FEARS

"I learned that courage was not the absence of fear, but the triumph over it. The brave man is not he who does not feel afraid, but he who conquers that fear."
–Nelson Mandela

How many times have you been married? One? Good for you. Two? Great. I'm happy for you.

How many times have you been to rehab? None? Congratulations! That's amazing. How many times have you been to jail? Oh, none, also good for you.

Yes. I've dealt with all those things. That doesn't make me cool or mean that I've been through more than anyone else. It just means I've had shit to overcome. We all have. Here's the thing: What have you been through? It doesn't have to be extreme like those, but you have to go through something; you have to overcome some type of adversity to be able to appreciate the wins you're going to have in life.

The first time I was married, it lasted forty-four days. I came home from my honeymoon and was given a list of shit I needed to fix. I thought it was going to be things like the sink and the closet door, but it was not. Oh... and the list was on a fancy-ass Post-it note. It was things that I needed to fix about myself. *Fix me? WTF!* There is nothing wrong with me. Everything is everyone else's fault, right?

There was also the demand that I had to stop working with my grandfather. Uh... no. Have you met me? Do I suddenly seem like someone who is going to do that to the man who raised me? GTFO.

I also had to stop drinking, which, in hindsight, was probably a good suggestion, but that wasn't how I felt when I was twenty-one years old. That was never going to happen.

I was actually told I had to stop cursing. My response to that was, "You can go f*ck yourself." So, that was the end of that relationship forty-four days into that experiment. Now, to be fair, I'm guessing she remembers things differently than I do. I'm guessing that I was a total f*cking nightmare and that getting out of that relationship was probably the best and healthiest thing for everyone involved. But I was full of anger and fear and just wanted to burn shit down.

The second time I got married, I've got to tell you, I had a party on the forty-fourth day. I thought that we were in the clear, but then you know what happened? Alcoholism, drinking, and a lot of drugging. I was not the person I was supposed to be yet. I had a ways to go. Obviously, I didn't know that at the time. I just thought I was being wronged. Again... couldn't be me. I'm great. Yeah, I might screw up once in a while, but who doesn't? Everyone gets a DUI here and there. Everyone drinks daily and hides it, right? Right? The booze and drug abuse became a very large problem, so that marriage ended after about a year and a half.

After that, I gave up. I assumed that my life was pretty much over. Who the hell would want me now? My dream of having a family had been snuffed out. I was a drunk and an addict; somehow, even though I did cocaine daily, I was fat as hell. I still haven't been able to do the math on how that worked. Then came the worst/best day of my life.

After spending eighteen hours drinking and doing drugs, I got pulled over for going the wrong way down the street at two a.m. and charged with my fourth offense, a felony DUI—and I narrowly dodged some very, very severe drug charges.

I was looking at one to five years in prison, and my lawyer told me, "If you go to rehab, you might be able to lower that sentence. It's not a foregone conclusion by any stretch of the imagination, but it's a higher likelihood that you won't get one to five years in prison." And remember, I was this three-hundred-ten-pound pile of shit at the time.

So, I ended up going to rehab with the intention of trying to get out of the consequences—that was it—and I was there for thirty days total. I tell everyone who asks that it doesn't matter how you get to rehab as long as you get there. I was not there to get clean. However, by the time I left, I had changed.

I don't really remember the first week and a half—they were a blur— but I do remember how, at about the halfway point, I was sitting in a lecture hall, looking around the room, and I could see all these plates, chairs, cups, and stuff on the wall. You'd get a plate if everyone in your group went to AA meetings that week, and you got a cup when you came back after a year of sobriety.

I just completely zoned out. I remember looking out the window and seeing all the snow on the ground and thinking about how damn cold it was and how I felt like I was never getting out of there. I couldn't hear anything that the person lecturing was saying at the front of the room. Then, from out of the blue, I said, "Holy f*ck. I'm in rehab."

The entire place went silent, and everybody looked at me like I was f*cking out of my mind—like, *what's wrong with this guy?*

I had this moment where I realized, "Dude, normal people don't go to rehab. Normal people don't have to come to a place like this. Maybe you've got a problem. Maybe you have something that you need to face." So, I decided to listen to people. I needed to shut the f*ck up and listen.

I was afraid of everything. I was afraid of failure. I was afraid of people. I was afraid of relationships.

I didn't feel like I could trust anybody. I remember sitting in the kitchen at the facility, and one of the patients had his family there—I think his wife was there. We were sitting at a table and having a conversation, and she was asking me about my life and my family, how I'd lost everything that I'd lost, and what I hoped for in the future.

I just looked at her and said, "I'm thirty years old. I'm overweight and divorced twice. Who the f*ck would want me? Nobody."

Why would anybody want to be a part of that f*cking baggage? All I ever wanted was to have my own family, to have a wife who gave a shit about me, and to have a kid I could help raise who was my own and have them to love and to have them love me. I never thought that would be possible. I had no idea that a year and a half after I got sober, I would meet the woman who would become my wife.

For whatever reason, she saw past all of that shit. She saw past all of my past. She saw me as the person not only that I was, but the one that I could be. Well, either that or I tricked the shit out of her. I guess I should ask her about that.

I was given this opportunity to have the family that I had always dreamed about, and today, I have the most amazing daughter and wife that anybody could ask for. It doesn't mean that they aren't a pain in my ass sometimes, but I have the life that I was begging for fifteen years ago. I genuinely consider myself one of the most fortunate people I know.

There are still times today when I complain and bitch and moan about what I don't have. But back then, I would have given anything to have the life that I have today. I would have given my left nut to have HALF of what I have today. And I don't mean financially. I mean spiritually, emotionally, all of it. Yeah, I have a great home. Yeah, I've got a kick-ass truck. But better than that, I have amazing people in my life. I have friends who genuinely care about me and what happens to me. They aren't looking to see what they can "get" from me. They are checking in to see how life is going, how they can help, and how we can participate in each other's lives. Dude... that's amazing.

Are you checking in on how great you have it, even though you are still on your journey? Do you take a daily inventory of what you're grateful for? If not, why not? It takes five minutes. Try it. Your life will change.

The point of saying all that is that you have to love what you went through.

I appreciate my life more now than anyone who hasn't been through shit like that. You've got to love what you went through. There's no reason to regret it. You have to have yin to have yang. You can't identify good if you don't know what evil is. You can't fully appreciate wins without losses. You get it.

I will actually take time to say thank you to that old me. I do this because, without that old me, I couldn't have the new me. I wouldn't be able to help the people in recovery get sober today without all the shit that I went through. Who would listen to someone who hasn't done anything? Do you know why I hated college? Because not one of my professors had ever actually done anything in life except read books. They read a book and then tried to tell me how to live it in the real world. Piss off. Go accomplish something. Fail. Get back up. Fail. Get back up. Do that over and over again... Then come teach me something.

Now, again, that doesn't mean that I am glad that I hurt all the people in my past. Of course not. Of course not.

But without those experiences, I wouldn't be the person that I am today. What I want you to know is that you can't win unless you fail. I just got done filming a podcast of *Be Authentic or Get the F*ck Out,* and we spent an hour talking about the fact that you don't learn anything from wins.

Well, that's not true. You learn that you really like winning, but you don't actually learn anything else. Every success that I've had in my life is directly related to some type of adversity and facing some kind of fear.

So, when you do fail, the question is, what do you do with the information? What do you do with the loss? Do you just say, "Well, that didn't work," and then that's it? Or do you actually dissect it, go through it, do a debrief, and figure out the things that didn't work? The truth is, you're never starting over from scratch. You're starting at a completely different place in a timeline and knowledge line because you have all of this information.

You just went to school for however long it took you to have that failure because it is a lesson. Then, if you take that lesson—actually take actionable steps based on what went wrong so that you can change your actions the next time—and you rinse and repeat that over and over again, you are going to win. But you have to be able to face that fear of failure and overcome the adversity that you're dealing with at that moment.

You have to understand that losing is winning. I've never been given anything. People think that I was given a business because my grandfather started it back in the '60s, and I started working with him at a very young age, but that's bullshit. He sold me a one-man show with no processes, no systems, and no people. It was two guys with a job, me and him, and my grandma answering the phones and doing the books.

Now, I did get a name that a few people knew, and that was obviously worth something, but I wasn't given anything. I decided to build an actual business out of that. And I wanted to build it out of that because I wanted to make sure that I protected my grandfather's legacy, as he had overcome so much adversity in his life.

He had absolutely nothing when he started. He had fifty dollars in his pocket, a truck, and a tar kettle to put on the old asphalt tar roofs. I wanted to honor that legacy by keeping his name for our business and making sure that when I hang it up, that name continues to live on. I decided to build an actual business. I worked on roofs and have the tar scars to prove it. I was up on those roofs until I was twenty-nine years old.

As of the writing of this book, I'm forty-five. *Oof*, man, I wonder if we could edit that out. I don't want to be forty-five. That's okay; we'll keep it here. I worked on roofs until I was twenty-nine years old. Not many company owners have done that, but I'll tell you what—the ones who have actually worked in the trenches of their businesses and learned how to get out of the trenches to truly own a company are generally the most success-ful. They're mostly old-school guys.

A lot of the young guys coming into business don't have that. I feel bad for them, to be completely honest, because I think you have to get kicked in the ass. I think you have to get bullied on a job site. I think you have to get yelled at and made to feel like shit every once in a while for doing things the wrong way to be able to grow those scars and learn what doesn't work. I learned from watching my grandpa accidentally show me what doesn't work so that when I did take over the company, I was able to make the changes and say, "I don't want to work that kind of hard my whole life. I want to work a different kind of hard. Smart and hard."

We have to try new things. We have to get uncomfortable—and getting uncomfortable is scary. But the thing is, the more things you do that are scary, the more opportunities will come your way.

I talk about this all the time when I go to conferences. Whether I'm there for my podcast or to speak on a stage, every time I go, when I get there, within twelve hours, I check flights to see if I can find one that leaves earlier so that I can just go home. I'm uncomfortable; I don't want to be there. I want to be at home with my family. I'm safe there. I can't be embar-rassed. I can't be ignored or rejected.

I do the same thing at retreats because it's a little scary being around people you don't know. You don't necessarily know what's going to happen. You don't know who you're going to be talking to. You don't know where the conversations are going to go. Whenever I have those feel-ings—and this is probably one of the hardest skills that I've had to learn over the years, being self-aware—I know that that is the moment that I have to lean into the uncomfortable because I'm going to get so much out of it. I know that opportunities are going to come my way because I'm going to lean into that discomfort.

No one has ever done anything remotely f*cking cool playing it safe, and if they have, I don't want to be friends with them. Those people are boring as shit. Every single person who's done anything of consequence took risks, and usually, they got their asses handed to them at least once or twice.

I always speak in sports analogies, but no one has won a championship in sports by calling it in at practice, just going through the motions, and then showing up on game day and performing. They bled. They wanted to quit. They wanted to give up, take their ball, and go home. They wanted to call their mom, but they didn't. Like Dory from the movie *Finding Nemo* said, they just kept swimming.

They kept f*cking going—every single day. It was hard. They got their ass kicked. They got back up. They got their ass kicked again. They got back up.

I only relate to people who have overcome adversity because it means they put themselves out there. They were okay with the fact that they might end up looking like a dipshit if things went wrong. I love those people because they don't give a f*ck what people say about them. They're going to continue to take risks. You have to take risks.

Now, fear is the opposite of acceptance. If you accept that whatever happens is what is supposed to happen, there's nothing to be afraid of. It's just an outcome, and now you have to decide how to proceed moving forward.

Now, I have been given the gift of learning this because of my decades of sobriety, but I never used to choose to accept anything. I always had to manipulate. I always had to figure out a way to make things go the way I thought they needed to go. Then, if they didn't, I would blame somebody. I'd make sure that it was somebody else's fault if it didn't go exactly the way that I'd f*cking scripted it.

Finally, I learned to accept things and that whatever happens is what is going to happen; it just is. When we accept that everything just IS, our only responsibility is to figure out what we're going to do with that information. How are we going to react? We can choose to be angry, or we can choose to be happy.

We can choose to see a problem as an opportunity to find a solution, or we can see it as just a problem and shut down. I was just having a conversation with my buddy Collin Schwartz on my podcast, *Be Authentic or GTFO*, about waking up in the morning and having a flat tire.

Now, you could go outside, see your flat tire, and say, "Motherf*cker! My whole day is ruined. Now what am I going to do? Better call my assistant and shut everything down. This is going to take the day."

You could also come out, look at it, and say, "Well, at least it's only one tire."

Or you could come out, look at it and go, "Man, I am so fortunate that I have people in my life who are here to help me when I have a flat tire. My wife can take the kids to school, and I can get the car to the dealership and get this tire fixed. All I have to do is move a couple of things around, and everything's going to work out. Man, I'm lucky."

What an amazing perspective that third person has. He'd chosen not to let the flat tire ruin his day. Instead, he's looking at it through a different lens so he can help himself and others instead of complaining and just giving up.

Do you see how that same situation can be seen in so many ways? If you live in that fear, you become crippled. You can't make decisions in that high or low state.

Instead, we have to be in a state of zero. If we're too high, excited, and happy about something, we're probably not going to make the best decision because we think nothing can go wrong. Because of this, we're not analyzing the situation properly to ensure that we're making a good decision. And if we're in a low, negative state, then we'll think nothing can go right and everything is going to fail.

You have to figure out how to get yourself back to zero. But if you learn to live in that state of acceptance, then you don't have to go high or low because you know that whatever happens is what's going to happen.

There's an old Chinese proverb that I absolutely love that completely changed how I see things. It illustrates the idea that many events can't be judged as good or bad until time has passed.

The story goes like this. A farmer's son locks the stable gate behind seven horses, and their neighbors congratulate the farmer, saying that he'll be able to maintain the farm with three horses and sell the rest for profit.

Everybody is so happy for him, but the farmer replies, "Maybe yes, maybe no."

The next day, the farmer's son breaks his leg while breaking in one of the horses. All the neighbors come running, and they're so sad, saying that the farmer is no longer going to be able to count on his son's help. They're going to lose all their money. To this, the farmer simply replies, "Maybe yes, maybe no."

The next day, the Imperial Chinese Army comes to conscript young men into the army. The farmer's son isn't taken because of his broken leg. When neighbors congratulate the farmer, saying his son has avoided certain death, the farmer replies, "Maybe yes, maybe no."

The moral of the story is that it's often how you look at things that determines their power over you. It also teaches us that life is cyclical. Good fortune can come from bad fortune, and bad fortune can come from good fortune, which proves that everything just is. It's not good or bad. Things just are. You make decisions based on your own belief system of what is good or bad. But if you start to see things as they are, acceptance can take over your life.

An example of this is every war that's ever been fought in the entire world. Everyone thinks that they are on the right side of history. I don't think there have been many rooms with Dr. Evil in the background going, "Ha, ha, ha, I'll show them. I'm the evil guy, and they're the good guys." No one is writing a storyline like that in their war rooms.

Hitler thought he was right. He thought he was doing the right thing for his people. Now, I am not going to say that Hitler was right about anything; obviously, that's not the case. But he thought he was. Going back and changing history to stop what happened back then would remove the lessons that we learned from it to become better people.

Now, I realize that this sounds f*cking horrible, and like I just said, I wouldn't go back in history and stop the Holocaust. That's not what I'm saying. What I'm saying is that everything just *is*, and we can't control it. However, we can choose what we do with the information and from the horrors that have happened in life. We have to accept them because there's nothing that we can do to change them.

So, what do you do with the information that you learned from something that did happen? Have your own thoughts and opinions on things because it's what you do with those opinions that defines who you are. Do you sit back and just watch everybody do shit or watch bad things happen and then do nothing about them? Or do you make changes in your life? The people reading this book are the ones who want to make changes in their lives.

Don't take that lightly. If you see bad shit happening, something that negatively impacts you, change the narrative. Learn something from it.

If you don't learn how to accept those things, you will constantly live in a state of anger and fear. Then what? You're going to attract people who live in the same state. That's not what we're trying to do here. We're trying to live in a state of acceptance. So, if you're always in fear or anger, everyone around you will be as well. This is obviously not healthy; it's not who we want to be, and it's not who people want to follow. They want safe, remember? They want stable. Are you safe and stable? How are you showing that?

This applies to both your personal life and your business life. You can't lead people in your company if you're constantly angry or fearful of what's going to happen next. If you are, they're not going to want to be around you, and they're not going to trust you.

And what's the "T" in the T.E.A.M. Method, folks? Trust. None of this works without trust. Build the trust of your people so that they believe in you to make the right decisions. The whole intent of this book is to help you grow the people around you, whether it's in your business or your personal life. If you're not an example of how you want them to be, they're going to follow your negative example instead.

If every time something happens that can be perceived as negative and I go around screaming and yelling and upset about it, everybody else in the office is going to see that. Everybody else in my life is going to see that. And they're going to be like, "Well, that's how Eric reacts to this kind of thing, so, obviously, it's okay if I react like that, too." Well, that's not what we want for them. They're watching us, so make sure that everything you do is what you want mirrored back to you—because it will be.

It's the same thing with your kids. If you scream at them, how do you think they will handle adversity later in life? Probably with anger, just like you. What if you slowed down, assessed the situation, made a proper choice, and explained that choice? Now, how do you think your kids are going to deal with adversity? Hey! Everyone is watching you! Everyone! You have a responsibility. Take it seriously.

Now, my biggest fear is being alone.

I know for a fact that one of the biggest reasons that I drank so much and used drugs was my fear of being alone. I wanted to be accepted, and I wanted to have connections with people. As an introvert—and I am a natural introvert—I didn't know how to do that.

Booze and drugs made that easier for me in the beginning. Eventually, though, no one wants to be around you because you're always a f*cking mess. Who wants to be around a mess all the time except for other messes? You are not going to get high-level people who want to spend time with you if you're constantly a piece of shit doing piece-of-shit things.

You have to want to be better. Whether it's our personal growth and development, our businesses, or whatever, we all hit different plateaus where we spend a lot of time with the same people and have maxed out what we're gaining from them and giving back to them.

Then, every once in a while, we get an opportunity to meet somebody new who reinvigorates us. That's constantly happening, and you have to always be on the lookout for it because the minute that you think you have it all f*cking figured out, you're done. Just dig your hole right now. You have to want to be better.

I lived in that state of fear when I drank. I feared that people would leave me, and then that would happen. Have you ever lived in a state of fear? If you get to a point in life where you don't have anyone around you to support you, you are living your nightmare. That was the nightmare I was living, and it's one of the reasons that I wrote this book.

I know that this book was written to help people build and grow their teams, make money, and all of those things, but I also want people to know that no matter where you're at on your path and how dark it is, there's always a way out, and other people have been through what you're going through. Please remember that negative emotions attract negative outcomes, and positive emotions attract positive outcomes.

This reminds me of a story. I hadn't seen a friend of mine in many years, and we got an opportunity to golf at my club. The college team that we root for was playing that day, and it was a big game, so I put it on my phone so we could listen to it while we golfed. As the game went on, our team was not doing well, and we started to get a little upset. Then, we started getting extremely negative.

Prior to that, I had been playing pretty well, but all those negative

57

emotions started to filter into my golf game. They started to filter into the quality of the time that I was spending with my friend.

We looked at each other, and I said, "Andrew, I'm going to turn this game off. Are you okay with that? Because I feel like the energy has just completely changed. Neither of us is playing as well as we normally do, and we don't seem to be having fun anymore. We don't need to listen to this shit. Let's enjoy the moment and be present in what we're doing."

"Yeah, man," he replied. "Turn off the f*cking game."

So, I turned it off, and the entire mood and trajectory of our golf game changed. Our whole attitude changed. We removed negative energy. I know that sounds hippy-dippy, but it's real, man. It's real. I ended up coming back and shooting my second-lowest round of the year at that course, all because I removed the negative energy.

We have to stay out of the negative. We have to push ourselves into the positive and choose how we want to see things because we get to choose. You get to choose. We need to be present and in a state of gratitude.

I've got a challenge for you because, as we talked about earlier, you cannot make decisions when you are high or low. You have to be in a state of zero because, otherwise, you cannot see the pitfalls or the possible things that could go right. So, you have to figure out how to get yourself to that calm state. What I'm going to suggest to you is to find a coach or an app to teach you how to meditate and breathe. Now, I know, to some of you, that will sound extremely basic and stupid.

I will share with you how this has completely changed my life. I did not know how to change my state, so I had to hire a coach to teach me how to lower my heart rate because, at the end of the day, that's what we're doing. We have to lower our heart rate, and we have to figure out how to do that.

I had to get hypnotized, and I had to have all kinds of crazy shit. I'm not saying that's what you have to do, but it took many, many months for me to learn how to change my state and then how to change it faster and faster and faster.

To give you an example, I'd bring up a situation to my coach that happened that day, and he'd ask me, "How did that make you feel?"

"I got really angry," I'd reply.

"How long were you angry?"

"Three or four hours. Then I was able to get over it and go back and make decisions."

Then, a month or two later, the same situation would happen, and he'd say, "Okay, what happened?"

"I got angry," I'd say.

"How long were you angry for this time?"

"About an hour. Then I was able to get back and make a good decision."

Another month or two would pass, and the same thing would happen. "Well, how long did it take you to get back to being able to make decisions?" he'd ask,

"I was angry for about five minutes," I'd reply, "but then I was able to get back on track."

That's what we're looking for, people. We're looking for incremental change. It won't happen overnight. You're going to have to put in the work to actually make it happen, but you can change.

Now, that is not the kind of coach I am. That is not what I do. I have learned that, and I can do it for myself far better than I used to be able to, but that is not the kind of coach I am. So, I suggest that you find that kind of coach or an app that will lead you in meditation to calm your mind down so you can get back to that zero place.

The other thing I would challenge you to do is, when you are feeling low, make a gratitude list. Write down ten things you are grateful for. It sounds stupid, but it will change your life and your outlook. You can't be pissed when you are in a state of gratitude. Try it. Tell me how it goes.

Shoot me an email at eric@ericoberembt.com and tell me how making a gratitude list for thirty days changed your life.

Transform Your Mindset in Just Thirty Days!

Gratitude has the power to shift your perspective, boost your happiness, and attract more positivity into your life. Scan the QR code for my 30-Day Gratitude Worksheet to track your daily moments of thankfulness and see the difference it makes!

SIX
MEANING AND EXPERIENCES

"The purpose of life is to live it, to taste experience to the utmost, to reach out eagerly and without fear for newer and richer experience."
– Eleanor Roosevelt

I talked about my grandfather in a previous chapter. What you have to understand about him is that he had no idea about the stage he would be setting for me all the way back in 1965 when he started our company, D&M Roofing. This was nineteen years before I was even born. I'm pretty sure he had no idea what would happen fifty years later with that one-man show that he started.

When I was seven years old, my parents got divorced, and we moved in with my grandparents. I was already close to my grandfather. We used to spend all kinds of time together. He would drive out to our house when we lived a state away in Iowa, and I would try to sneak into his truck to go back with him to Nebraska to spend the week or weekend with him. Fast forward, he basically became my dad. He took me to all of my practices. He took me to ball games, got my hair cut, taught me how to drive, and gave me my first beer.

Thanks for that, Gramp.

He taught me business, how to work hard, and how to sell. He also took me to the horse track, where I learned fractions. I was the only kid who knew what a three-to-two bet paid on two dollars when I was eight years old. He literally taught me everything that I knew. He was my grandfather, my father, my mentor, and my best friend.

4-year-old Eric in the Roofing Truck. Just getting started.

When he passed away, it left an extremely huge hole in my heart. I didn't have that person anymore to talk to. Yeah, I was married, and I loved my wife, and we talked, but it just isn't the same.

I miss him literally every day.

My grandfather also taught me what it was to be a good human being. He taught me about helping other people. He had his own company, but he wasn't exactly raking it in. He made enough money to support his family—and he did an amazing job at that—but he wasn't able to save or put money in a retirement account. He didn't have "extra cash" lying around, but when someone needed a meal, they came to my grandpa's house because they always knew that he would have enough and would help them out.

When somebody needed a loan to help pay rent, they came to my grandpa. When someone needed a job, he figured out a way that they could work on a crew. When someone needed somewhere to sleep, they came to my grandpa, and he never said no. This is who he was. He helped people in the way that he was able to. It was on a micro level, but it's how he made a difference.

This is how he gave meaning to his life, and this is what he taught me. He taught me to help when I can, but especially when I can't. If you don't think you have the ability to do it, do it anyway. It will come back to you.

This is what I learned as I started growing my company, as I had opportunities to help people on a micro level. I had opportunities to teach them things and grow them as humans. I saw it happen on a smaller scale, and I wanted more. So, I started going out and speaking on stage, and I also started my podcast.

I wanted people to feel that they were understood, that their struggles were understood. We need to create meaning in people's lives so that they want to continue to be around us. This is extremely important in our businesses because what we're trying to do here is to grow a team.

We're trying to grow teams that want to stay in our organizations forever, right? We want to make it so that they have no reason to want to go anywhere else. Well, the only way that we can do that is to make sure that they don't feel like a number.

I went to college for a few years, and every time I went to a new class, I was identified by my Social Security number. And I remember just how weird that felt because nobody really gave a shit about me. Nobody really cared about what my name was or who I was or allowed me to give context to my answers or projects based on things that I might be going through. I was just a number.

If your team feels like a number, if the people around you feel like numbers, they're not going to feel like they're part of anything bigger than themselves. So, you have to figure out how to make them feel like you care about what they care about.

You have to give meaning to their work and show them how it's helping other people, or they're not going to stay. You also have to show them that, again, you care about what they care about, right? How do you support them in their endeavors in life outside of work? Are you having these conversations with your people to find out what makes them tick? Or are you only focusing on them as an asset in the business? There's nothing more satisfying than seeing someone thrive in your life or your organization.

You can see the ones who have a passion for what they do. My suggestion is to ask them what gives them that passion. Is it financial goals? Is it something to do with their family? Or is it something else? If they make a certain amount of money, maybe they're able to help a certain amount of people.

Make sure that your team knows that everything you do is so that you can give back a certain amount of our proceeds to charities, like Roofers in Recovery and charities for veterans. We do a veteran roof giveaway every year to somebody who's in need and can't afford to put a roof on their house but needs to right now. And everybody gets behind that and understands that the more money that the company generates, the more people we're able to help.

So, we have to find out what our people need. Another example that I think you might be able to relate to is how, after my daughter was born, my wife quit her job and decided to stay home to raise her, which was what we both really wanted. She then decided to work for our company doing accounting because that was her background and she was really good at it.

You could tell, though, that she was missing passion and she was missing a purpose because the main purpose was our daughter, which is amazing. But we sat down one day, and we talked about it, and I said, "Teegan is only going to be young for a certain amount of time. Eventually, she's going to grow up. So, what gives you passion?"

We discovered that it was fitness and nutrition—it was helping other people at the gym. She started studying fitness and nutrition, and she learned that she loved helping people who were trying to achieve the same health goals that she was. Then she got the opportunity to coach my daughter's soccer team and help all the girls on her team become better players. She had played soccer all the way through college and had always been a part of a team. I could tell she missed that. Now I see her eyes light up every time she talks about coaching those kids. Every day, she gets to go to the gym and help people there work out. It's like she's a different person. Seeing that is so exciting.

So, how do you figure out how to give your team purpose and ignite that excitement and fire inside of them so that your business can prosper? You have to get them to buy into your vision and make it their vision and help them see that larger impact on the business, your customers, and other people who will be impacted. This means that we have to know what our revenue is going to do beyond just monetary gain. What can we do with that money? Who else can we help? Is being alive just about us and our goals, or is our purpose in life to change the people around us?

We all want to make as much money as humanly possible, but what are we doing with that money? What impact will it have? Personally, I like to use my money for experiences. I think experiences are one of the most important things that we can have in our lives and that we can give to other people.

It shocks me how many people haven't left their hometown and haven't seen the world at all. There is so much out there that we don't know about, so many places we haven't seen. I think we are meant to experience as much of the world as we possibly can, to see how other people live so we can appreciate what others go through and understand their challenges. This doesn't mean we can fix all the problems in the world, but it does mean we can learn and have empathy.

When my daughter is an adult, I don't want my daughter to look back and remember how all we did was go to soccer games and stay in the same town her whole life, how she didn't get to experience other cultures, countries, or people. This is why I make sure that a certain amount of our income goes to a fund for multiple vacations a year. That education and those experiences are the things that we're going to remember.

Yeah, this book is about creating a team that's going to be around for a long time, but it's also about creating moments in people's lives that stick with them. We want them to realize that these moments wouldn't have been possible anywhere else. And it's not just about taking your sales team on a retreat every year. It's about what they are experiencing on that retreat. Are you leading them through some amazing exercises and experiences that are giving them an opportunity to become a better person and help them become happier in what they're doing and in their life in general? Are you giving them meaning to what they do? Are you giving them meaning in their lives? Are you giving them the opportunity for experiences?

Find out what experiences they care about and make a blueprint for how they can do these things. Maybe their dream is to go to Hawaii; they've never been on a vacation like that before. How do we get them there? Are we sitting down and figuring it out? I'll sit down with my people and say, "This is exactly what it's going to cost you to go to Hawaii for two weeks with your wife. How do we get you there? Let's work the problem backward. I'll take a certain amount out of your check if you want me to and save it for you because I want to see whatever it is that you want to see happen."

If we're creating meaning for our people at work, the ripple effect is that they bring that positive effect to their home. If they come to work and they're happy every day, if they know that they're appreciated and that what they care about matters, they're going to be better able to positively impact people at home. This, in turn, helps the business because we need to create raving fans at home to be high performers and high-level leaders at work.

If our employees' spouses are not raving fans of our business and the way that we treat people, our employees will not stay with us very long because, every day that they go home, they'll be told, "Hey, are you looking for anything new? I see how miserable you are." If we get our employees' buy-in, however, their enthusiasm will influence their spouses as well as the rest of their family members.

Our goal here is to retain teams, so we don't just need buy-in from the people in our organization; we need buy-in from the people our team members care about—their families. If we're having a Christmas party or any kind of retreat or event, I always thank the spouses for their support first. I always remind them how much they influence the people that they love—the people on my team. We have to make sure that they're bought in and that they see the meaning and the higher purpose behind what we're doing on a daily basis.

A book that I would recommend reading once you're finished with this one is *The Happiness Advantage* by Shawn Achor.

In a nutshell, *The Happiness Advantage* says that you don't do things and then become happy. You have to decide to be happy so that all the good things that you want will come to you. People are attracted to other people who are happy and content—whatever word it is that you want to use that resonates with you.

If you show up and think, *If I can just close this deal, then I'll be happy,* generally speaking, it's not going to work out. People are going to feel that energy. But if you come in and you've already decided that you're good regardless of the outcome, people are going to feel that, too, and they're going to want to work with you. This goes back to how we attract people into our lives. If we are living in a negative space, if we are living thinking that things aren't going to work out for us, they're probably not.

A lot of people have said this before, but we are the stories that we tell ourselves. If we tell ourselves that none of it matters and we can't win, then we're probably not going to succeed. We need to understand who we're trying to attract and that the only way that we're going to do that is if we're in the same space.

Again, it's our responsibility to figure out what that means for each person in our lives—our teams, our spouses, our kids, everybody. But it's our responsibility to figure out what that means for each person.

If you can help put that into their lives—again, you can't do it for them, but you can help them find a way to do it so they can be fulfilled and happy by default—why would they want to go anywhere else? It's going to increase everything that they do on a positive level. Keep your focus on the greater good and help those around you feel it and see it.

They need to feel that they are happy before any outcome even happens. Another trick that I learned is that if it doesn't happen, if the outcome that you were hoping for doesn't occur, if you're truly okay with it, they're going to feel that, too. I've had numerous business deals come back to me because the other person could see that I was fine and that my life was not going to be dictated by this one deal, and they wanted to work with somebody like that.

You get to choose whether to show up every day with a positive or negative mindset. Your whole life is a choice, and every challenge is an opportunity to solve a problem. But do you see challenges as opportunities, or do you just see them as more things on the list of shit you have to do? Now, I'm not the one who invented this saying, but everything that you do on a daily basis, you get to do.

You get to do it. Never say, "Oh, I have to do this." You get to do it because you're here. We are so lucky to even be alive. Entrepreneur and author Gary "Vee" (Vaynerchuk) talks about this a lot... but the chances of us being alive are one in four hundred trillion. Read that again: one in four hundred trillion. You are special. You are here for a reason. You have an opportunity to make a life and make a living and make a difference in other people's lives. Don't waste this opportunity.

You have an opportunity to have a family. You have an opportunity to have friends. You have an opportunity to work. Not everybody has that opportunity. You get to do those things, but you need to choose how you're going to show up. It doesn't mean that it's easy, but it is simple.

I always relate this to my sobriety. It is not hard to get sober, but it is really hard to stay sober. Staying sober requires making a choice every single day. Am I going to drink today? No, I'll worry about tomorrow, tomorrow. I can't control what the future will hold, but I can control the choices I make today, so today, I choose not to drink. Today, I choose to treat my people with respect. Today, I choose to be understanding of what others are going through. Today, I choose to care. Today, I choose to be patient with my wife and daughter. Today, I choose to be better. Today, I choose to learn. Today, I choose to show up even though I might not feel like it.

So, what choices are you going to make today? Worry about tomorrow, tomorrow. Be in the present. Tell yourself: *Today, I'm going to focus on the things that put meaning into my life.* The next day, wake up and make another choice. Do you want to be a prick today? Or do you want to show up and try to help as many people as you can?

Here's a challenge: I want you to sit down and actually have a one-on-one conversation with your people. Now, you can do this with your people at home, and you can do this with your people at work.

The example I'm going to give you first is doing it with your people at work. You can do this in group meetings, but if you do it one-on-one, it's more impactful. I do it with my direct reports and then have them do it down the line.

Sit down with them and find out what gets them up in the morning. Ask them, "What gives you purpose? What do you care about?" If they don't know, try to explore it. Ask them questions about what and who they care about. What's happened in their life in the past that has made them who they are today? Maybe they want to help other people who are going through the same thing that they did, so let's find out what those things are.

Make a list of everybody in your organization. A lot of them are going to have similar answers. Some are going to have crazy one-offs that other people don't, but start lumping all these things together so that you can have somebody take ownership of this. Maybe it's you if you have a smaller organization, but if you're a larger organization, give somebody the responsibility to put together what all these people care about and find out how the organization can give back to help them.

How can we give back? We already talked about what that looks like for me: I want to help people in recovery. For others in my organization, it might be dogs. They might care about some dog charity. While writing this book, I've decided that I want to start a new charity. I want to create a scholarship fund in my grandfather's name: the Delton D. Mares Memorial Scholarship. We are going to raise money to award to someone who wants to go into the trades. My grandfather barely finished the eighth grade. He started roofing as a teenager and turned that into his life's work. He changed lives because he learned a trade skill that others couldn't do. We are losing those skilled people, and I want to make sure that kids who aren't built for traditional four-year college (which I think is a joke anyway) are able to learn a skill and make a living so they can give back to others.

We need to show people that we care about what they care about because those people matter to us. On a personal level, you might not know what the people closest to you deeply care about, and the art of conversation has been lost, right? We need to get back to having conversations and finding out what makes people tick.

Take note of what that is. Have one-on-one conversations with people and actively listen to them. Actively listen to what other people are saying. Again, it's okay to take notes. Literally, write things down so that they know that you care about what they're saying.

In a business setting, I take notes while they're talking, and they'll look at me like I'm crazy. They'll ask, "What are you doing?"

"I am taking notes because I want to make sure that I am highlighting the things that are important to you," I'll reply. "Because what might be important to me might not be important to you. So, if we're going to work together, I want to make sure that I write down what you care about so that I can make sure that I cater this experience to you. I care about what gives you meaning."

SEVEN
CONNECTION

"We have a strong instinct to belong to small groups defined by clear purpose and understanding— 'tribes.' This tribal connection has been largely lost in modern society."
– Sebastian Junger

About four or five years ago, my coach, Clay Moffat, asked me to go on a trip to Mexico and have an experience with him. I can't expand on what it was that we were doing together because he likes to keep that private. What I can tell you is that I was hypnotized for basically six hours a day for two and a half days. (If it wasn't six hours, it felt like it.)

I went on this trip and allowed myself to be hypnotized for several days for a lot of different reasons. I was trying to build a better version of myself, to realize the things that I wanted to do with my life, and to learn how to implant certain ideas into my brain to be able to accomplish those things and feel certain ways. But I didn't really know all this when I showed up.

I trusted this man. Remember how important that is, trust? I trusted that whatever he was bringing to the table would be worth the extremely large amount of money that I was spending to do this thing.

On the first day, he asked me a simple question: "What do you want?"

I came up with a bunch of generic bullshit answers: money, revenue goals, and things like that. But I didn't really know the answer to the question. Finally, I said, "I don't know what I want."

"Okay," he replied. "That's fine."

So, we'd spend the day working together, being hypnotized, doing all these different woo-woo deals. Again, keep in mind, I did not believe in any of this woo-woo shit before I met my coach. He helped me get out of my comfort zone to really acknowledge and accept that there are a lot of things that you can do in your life to help you that you are not aware of, but you have to trust somebody to lead you through it.

For the entire first day, I wasn't able to talk, and I wasn't allowed to hear other people speak. So, if I wanted food, he would have to go get it for me and bring it back to the house.

On the second day, he asked me again, "What do you want?"

Once again, I replied, "I don't know. I don't know what I want."

So, we kept working through stuff. Finally, we got to the last day and started our session, and he asked, "Have you learned anything from these last two days? What do you want?"

Then I realized that the same word kept coming up over and over and over again: "connection."

All I wanted was a connection. I wanted a better connection with my spouse. I wanted a better connection with my kid. I wanted a better connection with all the people I deal with on a daily basis in my organization. I wanted a better connection with my friends.

I realized as well that all the struggles and addictions in my past, all of my bad decisions, were all because I was trying to find a connection. I would drink and use drugs because I felt like it would make people like me more. I felt that if I had enough drugs to give people, it would make them want to be around me, and I wouldn't be alone.

I just wanted a connection. I wanted people to see me. I didn't want to hide in the back corner of the room anymore. I wanted to be part of the room, part of the things that were going on, but I didn't know how to do that because I was scared to talk to people. I was scared to have all these conversations that we talked about in the previous chapters.

The reason for this was that I didn't know what the outcomes of those conversations would be, and that scared me. I didn't understand the concept of just accepting things as they are.

I just wanted to be close to people. Everything that we've been doing up to this point, everything that we talked about in the previous chapters, is to teach you how to gain a connection with other people. We all know that we are a tribal people, and we want to feel connected to others.

We know this instinctively, we know this educationally, and we know that this is a fact. Yet, more and more of us feel alone all the time because we don't have the connection that we're looking for.

We've all heard the phrase, "It's lonely at the top." Here is how I interpret that phrase. To me, it makes me think about how when we reach a level of leadership, we realize that everyone is looking at us for the answers. Generally, we have them. But the problem is that we don't always feel we have someone to ask when we have "the question." We don't have someone to talk to when we feel stressed or confused. We don't always have someone to lean on. That's why it's so important to make sure we are putting people in our lives that we CAN talk too. But when it comes to people inside your organization, it's only "lonely at the top" if you choose to be lonely.

This is one of the main reasons I started the "Cult Culture Movement" Accountability group. To make sure I and other people get a chance to surround themselves with other people in the same boat they are in and get to talk about it.

First annual "Exhale" Retreat in Grand Cayman. An amazing group of men.

Are you taking people along with you? Are you teaching them the things that we've talked about in this book? Are you following the blueprint that we laid out? Are you having conversations with your people? If you're doing all the things, if you're building trust, if you're showing empathy, if you're showing up as exactly who you are authentically and giving people in your life meaning in their lives, guess what? You're not going to be lonely, whether you're at the top or the bottom.

But remember, we can't always talk to people inside our organization about everything. We know that. We have to find people that we can lean on and who will support us in this journey so we can show up as the best version of ourselves for our people. And if you do these things, you're going to be at the top—whatever the top is for you.

Are you giving all these people a reason to trust you? Remember, trust is the foundation of this program, using the T.E.A.M. Method to create the team that you want to have in your life and your business. Are you building that trust by doing the things that we talked about? Connection is a culmination of implementing all the things that we talked about in the previous chapters.

I want you to read that again. **Connection is the culmination of working on all the things that we talked about in the previous chapters:** building a foundation of trust by employing empathy, authenticity, meaning, and better listening—in other words, shutting the f*ck up and listening better.

So, we've already talked about the fact that some energies will repel and others will attract organically, right? We have to remember that if we want to make connections, we need to make them with the people we're supposed to connect with. Now, that does not mean that it's just going to happen, right? You still have to put in the work.

You still have to put forth the effort. You're not just going to get out of bed, and things are going to happen for you, right? You can't stand by a shovel and think it's going to dig its own f*cking hole. You have to pick up the shovel and dig the f*cking hole. So, we have to do the work. We have to talk to people.

But who are we trying to connect with? We've talked about this in detail, and I realize that this is repetitive, but it's important because everything leads to connection. We want to make sure that we are attracting the energy that we want in our lives by putting out the energy and the connection that we want to get back.

If we are selfless in giving, then we can be selfish in receiving. The point here is that we want you to have the life that you want to live and also to give others the life that they want to live. None of that matters without connection.

It's about sharing our experiences with other people. Are we being vulnerable? There is no connection without vulnerability. I'm so glad that this is a book and not an audiobook because I don't know about you, but I can never say the word "vulnerability" correctly.

We have to be vulnerable to gain a connection with others. We have to talk about our experiences because shared experiences are what connect us. This is why soldiers and athletes have such strong connections. They are experiencing hard things TOGETHER. Who are the people that you have shared experiences with? Can you think how much closer you are to those people than you are to others? If what I'm saying is true, doesn't it make sense to try and make new experiences with people you want to make connections with?

What are experiences that we are willing to share with others? Personally, I share everything, probably to a fault. I tell everybody everything about my past, what made me who I am, how I used to deal drugs, how I was an alcoholic, how I went to jail, how I was a big, fat f*ck nobody wanted to spend any time with, and how I was alone. But then I also tell them what I did to overcome that.

I also talk to them about the steps I took so that I didn't have to be like that anymore because other people are probably going through some of the same things. So, share those experiences with people. Don't be afraid, and don't be selfish.

It is so selfish to keep those stories to yourself. If one person hears your story and changes how they operate or realizes that they're not alone and makes a change in their life for the better, it's all worth it. Think about it. If you didn't share that story, could they hear it from somebody else? Maybe, maybe not.

What if they didn't? And what if they didn't change their life? What if they kept going down the same shitty path because they thought that they were the only one, and their marriage failed and their business failed, and they lost their relationship with their kids all because you didn't want to tell your story because you were scared of people judging you? Be intentional about being genuine. Don't hide behind bullshit.

Don't hide behind your wins on Instagram. Live out front and embrace any failure that you might have had. Embrace the things that you've done to become who you are today because then you're not going to have to force connections with other people. They're going to naturally come to you.

When I go to events, usually, a lot of people want to connect and network with me. But the ones I connect with the most are the ones who don't force it because they're humble. They show up with a level of acceptance in their lives that whatever happens here happens. Let's talk to each other for a while and see how this works out. And if it doesn't, it doesn't. We're not going to try to force it. They're humble. They don't only talk about themselves. You'll never make connections with people if all you do is f*cking talk about yourself.

If you haven't learned anything else from this book, at least take this one thing: *stop talking so much about yourself.* Ask people more questions about who they are. Ask people more questions about where they're going. Ask people more questions about how they got where they are. Give them an opportunity to talk.

Now, here's the other trick. If you do that and you do it genuinely because you actually care about the other person, they will be able to feel that. The natural progression is that they're going to ask you to open up and tell you a little bit about yourself. That's how connection works, right?

People are often so self-absorbed that their conversations are all about themselves. Once the conversation ends, they move on with their lives. Generally speaking, these are not the people you want to associate with—unless you like people who only care about themselves. I don't. I like people who care about others.

So, that's one thing to look out for. You're going to have a really hard time connecting with other people if you are always trying to impress them. When you do that, you only shine a light on your insecurities. The guys who show up with the fake clothes and the fake cars and all the bullshit that we see on social media, we all know what they're insecure about. If they don't have any of those things, they think that they're going to be judged for that. That's the only way for them to feel successful, which is the saddest thing in the world.

Don't focus on what you want to portray to others. Focus on being authentic and genuine because that's when genuine and authentic connections will happen. Be real, be yourself, and be open to the connection. That's something that isn't talked about enough, but we have to be open to making connections with other people.

For the longest time, I used to put up really high f*cking walls to keep people out. I was afraid that if I let people in, I could be hurt.

We have to eventually tear those walls down and be open to having connections with other people because everybody's going to also feel those walls. That's the big thing I want everybody to remember: People can feel how you show up.

You can feel it when someone else is being insecure. You can feel it when somebody else is being fake. We've all got those "gut instincts."

You know that you do. So, why wouldn't everybody else? They do. They do have those gut instincts, too.

That's why you have to genuinely want to be available for the connection. This means that you genuinely have to be interested in what they're saying, and you have to ask questions to get to know them better, like we talked about.

If you can't genuinely be interested, you need to do a little more self-exploration to understand the why behind that. Why would you be so self-absorbed that you can't care about other people? We are put on this planet to interact with others. We are not here to be alone.

If you genuinely don't care about other people, maybe that means you're a sociopath or something. I don't know; I'm not a psychologist. But you need to do some self-examination to find out why. To be fair, everyone who got this far into the book cares about other people, so I'm really only talking to the people who got this far. So, be genuinely interested in what they're saying and ask questions. Realize that you also do not want to read off of a script.

That's the hard part of getting started on this if you are uncomfortable talking to people. I bring this up because I am. For a long, long part of my life, I have been very uncomfortable starting conversations with people to form these relationships and connections with them. At one time, I even told myself, *I just need a f*cking script. We all make sales scripts for our salespeople, right?* That's fine to get started, I guess. If you want to write down some questions just to put you in the right state of mind, go ahead.

Instead of that, I suggest listening more. Whenever I walk into a situation, if there's somebody I know I want to converse with or have a relationship with, I will listen to other people talk to them so that I can find out what it is that they already care about. Then I've got a question to ask, right? We don't go into the conversation asking, "What's your favorite color? What's your favorite number? Where's your favorite place to go on vacation?" Yuck, shut up.

Listen to them talk to other people if that's an option, and really hear what they're saying. Then you can jump in with a good question about that. "Why was that important to you?" Oh, they are talking about a vacation that they went on with their family to such and such island. "What was the most amazing part about that? What impacted you the most when you were there?" You just opened the door to a ton of shit that they could come up with.

People are going to know if you're just going off of a script. They can tell you're not being yourself. Here's another example of what you could do as a starter for a conversation. Ask them what question they get asked the most. Everyone you ask will know what their answer is. When I travel, the question I get asked the most is why I started the podcast. When I first started, honestly, I didn't know the answer. It took me a while to really figure it out.

The answer is that I started the podcast because I wanted to be able to get into rooms I might not have been able to get into otherwise and also have conversations with people whom maybe I normally wouldn't be able to. So, this was my cheat code to get people to actually sit down with me for an hour and have a genuine, authentic conversation so I could really learn about that person. If we connected, it gave me an opportunity to actually have a relationship with that person.

So, I started for selfish reasons, and now it's turned into something that actually helps other people because they get to learn from my guests' lessons. Now I know the answer to that question every time.

If I just gave you all of that information, you get to come back with, "Oh, my God, that's amazing. Who is one of your favorite guests that you learned the most from?"

"Oh, well, one of my favorite guests was Mark Lundholm because he's a famous comedian who's also in recovery, and he helps all of these different people across the country and the world with their recovery. And he goes to treatment facilities, and I resonate with him so much, and I would like to be a larger part of that community... *blah, blah, blah, blah, blah, blah.*"

"Oh, so why do you want to be part of that larger community?"

Do you see? It just goes on and on and on. To give, you have to be willing to receive, so you have to open yourself up to input. Open yourself to receive the information that people are giving you. It's not somebody else's responsibility to get you to listen. We also don't know how everyone expresses themselves.

Some people are extremely loud and flamboyant and have to be the life of the party, and other people are quiet and like to have one-on-one conversations with people. I'm the latter. So, if somebody tries to have a conversation with me in a large group of people, I tend to get a little more anxious, maybe a little bit more nervous, and I am not going to give the responses that I would like to give in the manner that I'd like to give them. Instead, I'll try to redirect the conversation, saying something like, "Hey, do you want to go hang out over there? We can bullshit over there a little bit because this is a little much for me."

If you still need to learn how to make better connections with people, I challenge you to join a networking group. Now, I'm sure most of you reading this have either already been a part of a networking group, have joined a networking group in the past, or are currently part of a group. My guess, though, is that you're not fully using it. You're showing up, you're eating lunch, you're talking to one person, the same person that you've talked to for the last year, or somebody you know who invited you to come to the event, and you're not really accomplishing anything.

You're not making new connections or relationships. So, I'm going to challenge you to force yourself to talk to three people you don't know without waiting for them to come talk to you first. Then I need you to take some notes. I need you to identify how it made you feel and acknowledge that. Be okay with it, right?

Maybe going up to someone new scares the shit out of you. Okay, that's fine. Acknowledge it, own it, and be okay with it: "Yep, it scared the shit out of me, but I did it anyway." That's called courage, folks. Just so you know, doing something that scares you and doing it anyway, that's courage. But identify how it made you feel and acknowledge it.

Be okay with whatever that feeling is. Maybe it excited you and made you feel more alive than you ever have. I don't know. But identify the positive opportunities that could arise from those three interactions: "I might be able to do business with this person. He's got thirty-two properties that could use my service." Whatever, identify all the positive opportunities that could arise.

Now identify how it made you feel, if it scared you, whatever the emotion was, and then compare it to the potential. My guess is that the potential of the relationship that you can make will outweigh the fear that's holding you back from doing it.

Again, I'm not just saying potential from a monetary standpoint. The potential could be making a really good friend: "This person seems like a really good human who cares about other people. Yeah, he might be able to help me in business, but he might also be somebody that I could actually talk to."

Next, you're going to write down the biggest thing that you can remember about each person you spoke to right after you're done speaking to them. This is extremely important. You've got to write this down because when you go back and talk to this person again, you're going to want to use it to reopen the connection.

I'll go a step further. If I grab their phone number, I'll treat it like a first date and, a few hours later, fire off a text message: "Hey, man, I appreciate you giving me your number and taking fifteen minutes to talk to me. I really enjoyed our conversation, and I look forward to getting to know you a little bit better down the road."

Take the time to do these things. Make notes—and not just mental ones. Write shit down. Whether it's on your phone or a piece of paper, write it down. If it's a business setting, explain to the other people present that you're doing it so that you can better serve them. Try this with your direct reports as well when you're having company meetings.

I suggest not taking notes when you're trying to form a personal connection with somebody—that's a little f*cking weird—but it's not weird when you do it in a business setting, like a sales pitch or working with your team. Please take the time to care about relationships and making connections with other people, and understand that all the work that we've done up to this point, all the things that we've talked about—how to create trust as a foundation, employ empathy with the people in our lives, show up as our genuine and authentic selves, and give meaning to the people around us—we're doing all of those things.

Why are we shutting the f*ck up and listening? We're doing it to build connections with others so that we don't feel alone, and neither do they. This is what it's all about.

CONCLUSION

"I did then what I knew how to do.
Now that I know better, I do better."
– Maya Angelou

As I said in the introduction, I wrote this book to talk to the "me" from fifteen years ago. Back then, I was scared and alone. I did not know how to connect with anyone, but I wanted to so badly. I tried so hard, and I ended up hurting so many people with my alcohol and drug use. I hurt my family, my friends, and numerous other people. Writing this book is my way of saying "thank you" and "I'm sorry" all at the same time.

I want people to know that I used all that pain to change who I was so that others could learn from my mistakes and not make the same ones. I truly pray that reading this will allow you to miss out on the shit that I felt and caused others.

Make your journey to the top, whatever that means for you, a little less painful. If you're going through anything, you have to know that you're not alone. You have to know that there are other people out there like you.

That's why we have communities. That's why I started the Cult Culture Movement and the Underwater Mastermind Exhale. It's why I love coaching. It's why I love speaking on stage and impacting large groups of people. It fills my cup.

I love helping people. It has made me who I am today. Giving back and being of service to others is what we were born to do.

Fifteen years ago, I did not know this. I thought that I was born to take care of myself. We were not born to be pieces of shit. We are supposed to help other people. What are you doing to help other people? Ask yourself that.

If you're not doing something to help other people, stop and figure out how you can. Also, ask yourself, why not? Do you think that you're not qualified to help other people? Sometimes, just listening can help other people. Sometimes, just showing up and being there can help other people.

You are talented and gifted at something. I don't know what it is, but you do. If you don't, just keep working at it. You'll figure it out.

You're talented and gifted at something, and you are a selfish prick if you aren't using that gift for the greater good. Use your gift and help other people. Again, if you don't know what it is, work hard to find out and then embrace it.

I want to thank all of you for trusting me and reading this book. This was not easy for me.

I thoroughly enjoy having deep conversations. I love speaking on stage and impacting large groups of people. This was different because I have so much to say, and getting it all on paper is not the easiest thing in the world.

But I took the time, and I did it for you. Everybody reading this is the reason I wrote it. This is not for me.

It is not for my ego. I want you to grow and become the human that you are supposed to be. Don't take that responsibility lightly.

People are looking at you. People see you as a leader in your business and your family. Don't let them down by not doing anything.

This shit is serious. After reading this book, you have so many things to start working on and implementing. Don't just finish this and think, *Hey, I read another book... cool.*

Take the time. Fill out the worksheets that are linked. Join a group.

I don't even care if it's mine. Just join a group where you can find support. They are everywhere. You just have to find the one that fits you. Find a coach. Find someone who can take you to that next level. When they do, find a new coach. Keep leveling up. Don't plateau. Keep moving. Eventually, you'll be buried six feet under, and you won't have the opportunity to do any of that. So, don't waste your f*cking time. Embrace life and get as much out of it as you can. You deserve it.

If you're interested in what we have to offer, check out CCM at www.cultureprogram.com. If you're looking for a community of people who support each other in life and business, please check us out.

Hit me up for coaching if you're going through something and need some special one-on-one time or if you want to get uncomfortable and go scuba diving and face some fears that only a small percentage of the world gets to do. And if you're an event director, I'd love to speak to your audience.

I love impacting people, changing lives, and making sure that people know that they aren't alone. We are in this together. Let's f*cking act like it.

And remember, if you really want to learn, we all need to shut the f*ck up and listen a little more.

THANK YOU FOR READING MY BOOK!

I would like to give you an opportunity to check out our accountability group "Cult Culture Movement" for free! Attend one call and see if you are a fit for the group. No one will try to sell you anything. I formed this group for entrepreneurs looking for people to hold them accountable for their lives.

Scan the QR Code Here:

I appreciate your interest in my book and value your feedback as it helps me improve future versions of this book. I would appreciate it if you could leave your invaluable review on Amazon.com with your feedback.
Thank you!